How the Way We Talk Can Change the Way We Work

How the Way We Talk Can Change the Way We Work

Seven Languages for Transformation

Robert Kegan

Lisa Laskow Lahey

JOSSEY-BASS
A Wiley Company
San Francisco

Jossey-Bass books and products are available through most bookstores. To contact Jossey-Bass directly, call (888) 378-2537, fax to (800) 605-2665, or visit our website at www.josseybass.com.

Substantial discounts on bulk quantities of Jossey-Bass books are available to corporations, professional associations, and other organizations. For details and discount information, contact the special sales department at Jossey-Bass.

TCF Manufactured in the United States of America on Lyons Falls Turin Book. This paper is acid-free and 100 percent totally chlorine-free.

Library of Congress Cataloging-in-Publication Data

Kegan, Robert.
   How the way we talk can change the way we work: seven languages for transformation / Robert Kegan, Lisa Laskow Lahey.
      p. cm.
   Includes bibliographical references and index.
   ISBN 0-7879-5535-3 (alk. paper)
   1. Change (Psychology) I. Lahey, Lisa Laskow, date. II. Title.
BF637.C4 K44   2000
155.2'5—dc21   00-010984

FIRST EDITION
HB Printing   10 9 8 7 6 5 4 3 2 1

Contents

3-29-01

Acknowledgments

We are deeply grateful to the thousands of people who have participated in the learning sessions that have led to this book, and especially to those who consented to have their experiences recounted here; for the love and generosity of our family members, Bill, Zach, and Max Lahey; Barbara Wolf, Lucia, and Josh Kegan; and to the following colleagues whose thoughtful and encouraging responses to earlier drafts helped us make a better book: Michael Basseches, William Drath, Catherine Fitzgerald, Ann Fleck Henderson, Robert Goodman, Gina O'Connell Higgins, Michael Jung, Emily Souvaine Meehan, Gil Noam, Laura Rogers, Christina Schrade, Elizabeth Speicher, James Wendler.

Emily Souvaine Meehan was especially helpful in revisions of Chapter Eight, and we owe the metaphor of the immune system to Michael Jung, who enhanced our own discourse. Finally, we would like to thank Karen Manning and Joelle Pelletier for their effective preparation of the manuscript, and our editor, Alan Rinzler, for heroic patience and wise counsel.

In memory of
William Graves Perry, Jr.

How the Way We Talk Can Change the Way We Work

What Do You Really Want . . . and What Will You Do to Keep from Getting It?

The late William Perry, a favorite teacher and precious colleague of ours at Harvard, was a gifted trainer of therapists, counselors, and consultants. "Whenever someone comes to me for help," he used to say, "I listen very hard and ask myself, 'What does this person really want—and what will they do to keep from getting it?'" This is a book about the possibility of extraordinary change in individuals and organizations. It locates an unexpected source of boundless energy to bring these changes into being.

As Bill's wry words suggest, if we want deeper understanding of the prospect of change, we must pay closer attention to our own powerful inclinations *not* to change. This attention may help us discover within ourselves the force and beauty of a hidden immune system, the dynamic process by which we tend to prevent change, by which we manufacture continuously the antigens of change. If we can unlock this system, we release new energies on behalf of new ways of seeing and being.

As developmental psychologists bringing the field of adult learning to organizational life, we are best known for championing the idea that there is life after adolescence; that our mental development, unlike our physical development, does not *have to* end at age twenty; that we can keep growing and developing in adulthood (and not just put on weight). A rich mix of professional groups—educators and administrators at all levels, managers and management consultants, physicians, psychotherapists, judges, and clergy—have afforded us unusual access to their deep-down inner purposes and puzzles. So when we are asked to consult or give counsel, it is nearly always because people know our focus is on the deeper, underlying changes in the way individuals and groups make meaning, rather than aiming for the immediate relief of symptoms or behavioral strategies to bring about short-term solutions.

Yet for all our occupational and preoccupational interest in the possibilities of transformation, we have developed a simultaneous fascination and respect for another aspect of our being, which can have the effect of *preventing* change. We have concluded that this dimension is not well understood in terms of "resistance," or "denial," or "fears," or "defensiveness," or "the shadow side of personality." Of course, each of these accustomed understandings triggers a stance—typically with unhelpful effects—regarding this very aspect of our being: people tend to say "How can we *break down* resistance—our own or that of others? How can we *overcome* our defensiveness? *Reduce* our fear?" And so on. In this book, by means of a new technology for learning (a "mental machine," in essence), we invite you into a novel and deeper understanding of this aspect of our being, one that is more respectful and consequently a more promising support to the miracle of individual and organizational change.

This book is for people interested in the possibility of their own transformational learning, as well as for people interested in supporting the transformational learning of others. We consider the second activity—widely practiced by helping professionals—an increasingly necessary feature of effective leadership, since nearly all leaders, in as dynamic a world as our own, are called upon to lead processes of change.

Leadership is a much more widely distributed and frequented activity than we are often given to believe. For every chief executive presiding at the top of some organization or enterprise, there are a thousand men and women called upon to exercise temporary or sustained leadership over a project or team within an organization. For every person assuming leadership because he or she sought to, planned to, and now does so as an extension of a long-crafted self-identity, there are countless others who lead because they were asked to; because "well, *somebody* has to"; because they were carried along, unsuspecting, by the momentum of their own interests, commitments, loyalties, and relationships.

However we come to find ourselves in these leadership roles, we are soon confronted with a set of daunting recognitions:

- Leading inevitably involves trying to effect significant changes.
- It is very hard to bring about significant changes in any human group without changes in individual behaviors.
- It is very hard to *sustain* significant changes in behavior without significant changes in individuals' underlying meanings that may give rise to their behaviors.
- It is very hard to lead on behalf of other people's changes in their underlying ways of making meaning without considering the possibility that we ourselves must also change.

Of course, we are not always aware of these as distinct and explicit principles. More often they show up as one conglomerate conclusion: despite our best efforts to lead for change, and sometimes even in spite of the sincere intention many of us have to change, very little significant change actually occurs!

This book is aimed at understanding better—and moving beyond—this discouraging conclusion. To help us do so, it introduces a "new technology" for personal learning. We do not use this overly familiar word to elicit the bells and whistles of the digital age (no PowerPoint presentation, no edge-of-the-seat suspense as to whether the next overhead will zoom in from the left or right side of the screen). Rather, we use it to recover its literal Greek origin, *techne,* which suggests the artful or skillful activity of making or building. We intend to help you build something in this book that can alter your relationship to change. This new technology is rooted in appreciation of three powerful forces in nature, which we briefly describe next.

When it comes to forces of nature, the most widely addressed and understood is what physicists call *entropy,* the process by which dynamic systems (such as people, organizations, automobiles, or solar systems) gradually fall apart. Entropy names the motion of increasing *dis*order, randomness, or dissipation of energy. Our bodies, our cars, our solar system, and of course our organizations are all wearing down. We could read Robert Frost's words in "Fire and

Ice" as an unconscious ode to entropy, wondering whether the earth will meet its end by a fiery collapse of its gravitational orbit or by the extinction of the sun itself—two fatal entropic processes, to be sure:

> Some say the world will end in fire
> Some say in ice . . .
> I hold with those who favor fire
> but if I had to perish twice . . .
> I know that for destruction ice
> is also great
> and would suffice.

Despite Frost's blasé attitude toward the prospect of being burned to a crisp or frozen into a block of ice, it seems unlikely that his heirs, some millions of years from now, will regard either prospect—should one eventually appear imminent—with quite the same equanimity. This brings us to consider two other, less well understood but equally important forces in nature.

Automobiles and solar systems cannot improve upon themselves, but people can. We can imagine, for example, that our fellow humans at some future time might spend generations in extraordinary action to depart the earth, were it to become clear that human life is eventually unsustainable here. Our orbit could be in decay, or the solar engine might well one day exhaust its fuel. But in the midst of these entropic processes we have the potential to organize ourselves at a whole new level of complexity, to become more ordered, to concentrate greater energy in our way of living that might permit us an extraordinary solution to our problem.

This is the very opposite of entropy, what physicists call *negentropy*. Our bodies *are* running down, but at the same time, with good luck and effective supports, our minds might be "running up." Our eyesight is deteriorating; we need corrective lenses as we age. But at the same time, our capacity to *see into* our situations and ourselves may become more acute; we may be able to discard previous psychological lenses of distortion or myopia. It is a distinguishing and heroic feature of living things that they participate not only in deteriorative processes of declining complexity, order, choice, concentration, and power but also in processes that lead to greater complexity, order, choice, concentration, and power. "We will never be able to solve our problems," Einstein said, "at the same order of complexity we used to create our problems."

Yet any of us who have deliberately sought to solve a significant problem—our own or that of some group we have sought to lead—knows it is no easy thing to set into motion the negentropic processes necessary to "solve our problems." We have the capacity to take extraordinary action at the individual or collective level, and yet more often we do not. The earth is not presently in danger of being incinerated by the sun, but it is in danger of being incinerated several times over by our own nuclear weapons. Human beings have never in their history constructed weapons they did not eventually use. We know this. Detonating these weapons would constitute a global entropic apocalypse. Disarming them would, as Einstein suggests, require a negentropic leap into some saving new way of reimagining our global conflicts.

Yet most important for the work we are about to undertake in this book, what we have today is neither detonation nor disarmament; neither the entropic nor the negentropic. This brings us to a third force in nature: the processes of dynamic equilibrium, which, like an immune system, powerfully and mysteriously tend to keep things pretty much as they are.

The forces that tend to keep things as they are may be a much greater player in the prospects of change than is commonly understood. Many leaders work toward accomplishing significant change—that is, negentropic change that moves their group or organization to a new level of capacity or complexity. Other leaders worry about their organizations losing their competitive edge and running down—that is to say, succumbing to the entropic processes of complacency, routinization, loss of focus, or dissipation of energy. But, as we hope to demonstrate in the pages ahead (using your own experience as the focus of attention), the biggest player standing in the way of an organization's chances to learn and grow might be the same force standing in the way of an individual's chances to learn and grow: this third force we call *dynamic equilibrium*.

Although it contrasts with processes of greater complexity and greater disorder, the third force is not about standing still, about stasis or inertia, about fixity or the lack of motion. As we are soon to see, this third force is *also* about motion. More precisely, it is about a system of countervailing motions that maintains a remarkably hearty balance, an equilibrating process continuously manufacturing immunity to change. It is possible to throw all kinds of personal and leaderly initiative at this dynamic equilibrium, often resulting in apparent change (losing ten pounds, realigning corporate attention), but the process of dynamic equilibrium eventually just throws out its enormous arms in response and before long waves itself back into familiar, upright balance (we regain the weight; the organization returns to business as usual).

There are countless books about personal change and leadership for organizational change. In one way or another, they recognize and warn against succumbing to the deteriorative drift of the entropic current. Such books can be tremendously appealing in championing the negentropic possibility of our moving against the tide. But as psychologists of adult learning and adult development, we wonder whether with just these two dynamic forces we have fashioned a sufficiently complex picture of the forces at work in our prospects for change.

Is any effort at personal change—our own or that of others we may seek to lead—likely to be powerful without better understanding of this third force in nature, our own immunity to change? Specifically, is change likely without grasping how this third force expresses itself in the unique particulars of our own lives? And yet, one of the things that makes gaining this understanding so difficult is that we tend to be held captive by our own immune systems. We live *inside* them. We do not "have them"; they "have us." We cannot see them because we are too caught up in them. This is precisely why a new technology for personal learning is needed. In this book, we present such a technology, built around the idea of transformative "languages"; it is a technology rooted in twenty years of research and practice as developmental educators.

How can we secure for ourselves the supports most likely to foster real change, change that actually escapes the immunizing gravity of our own dynamic equilibria and leads to new concentrations of energy, enhanced capacity, greater complexity? How can we as leaders for transformational learning better understand and exercise our own opportunities to create learning-rich settings for those we are privileged to have work with us and for us?

This book seeks to engage these questions by involving you directly in an immediate set of personal experiences. (You might do well to think of the first several chapters as the reflective equivalent of an Outward Bound ropes course.) The purpose of these activities is simultaneously to promote your own personal learning and to introduce you to a new technology designed to create enough cognitive and emotional "thrust" that you can at least temporarily win some distance from your own dynamic equilibrium.

The building blocks for this new technology are novel language forms. Each language is a tool, transforming a customary mental or social arrangement into a form that increases the possibility of transformational learning. The places where we work and live are, among other things, places where certain forms of speech are promoted or encouraged, and places where other ways of talking are discouraged or made impossible. We are referring to how we speak to each other in public and private conversation, in groups and informal one-on-one communication, and perhaps most especially (at least in the beginning) with those few others with whom we may feel the most trust and comfort.

We are also referring to how we speak to *ourselves,* which, though too rarely considered, is one of our most influential and continuous conversational venues. (Being psychologists, we can certify that, contrary to popular lore, talking to oneself is not a sign of being crazy; it depends on what we say to ourselves!) Here we are emphasizing less the content of what we say than the form in which our saying goes on. The forms of speaking we have available to us regulate the forms of thinking, feeling, and meaning making to which we have access, which in turn constrain how we see the world and act in it. Some language forms concentrate more individual and social energy than others do; they provide more focus, increase direction, and enhance capacity—in short, they may be tools toward negentropy. We know this may seem a rather abstract idea at the moment, but before long you will have a direct experience of seven qualitatively different language forms—internal and interpersonal languages—that, taken together, we believe increase the possibilities of our ongoing unfolding. In our experience, these novel language forms do not spring up on their own. They require intention and attention. A good gardener must plant them and help them grow.

This premise that work settings are language communities brings us to a corollary premise: all leaders are leading language communities. Though every person, in any setting, has some opportunity to influence the nature of the language, leaders have exponentially greater access and opportunity to shape, alter, or ratify the existing language rules. In our view, leaders have no choice in this matter of being language leaders; it just goes with the territory. We have a choice whether to be thoughtful and intentional about this aspect of our leadership, or whether to unmindfully ratify the existing drift of our community's favored forms. We have the choice to make much of the opportunity, or little. We have the choice to be responsible or not for the meaning of our leadership as it affects our language community. But we have no choice about whether we are or are not language leaders. The only question is what *kind* of language leaders we will be. This book can thus also be read as a kind of itinerary, arraying a variety of ways we may wish to be more enterprising in this aspect of our leadership.

The four chapters of Part One take you through a step-by-step process to build a customized version of a new technology, a new mental machine, for your own personal learning. Using four new languages as tools, you build a technology that gradually introduces you to your own immune system, your own dynamic equilibrium, the forces that keep the immune system in place, and the possibilities of transcending it. Each of the four transforms a customary internal psychological set or mental arrangement into a novel form:

1. From the language of complaint to the language of commitment
2. From the language of blame to the language of personal responsibility
3. From the language of "New Year's Resolutions" to the language of competing commitments
4. From the language of big assumptions that hold us to the language of assumptions that we hold

Taken together, they build a mental machine. If you value this machine, you will want to maintain it and upgrade it. The three chapters of Part Two introduce you to three more languages that explicitly serve these purposes. The question of how we can maintain and continuously upgrade a powerful means of personal learning is important to us not only as individuals seeking what we need for our own growth but also as leaders thinking about how to enhance dramatically the learning that goes on in our organizations. Each language in this second part transforms a customary interpersonal, social, or organizational arrangement into a novel form, both to support smooth operation of the new technology and to make it continuously improvable:

5. From the language of prizes and praising to the language of ongoing regard
6. From the language of rules and policies to the language of public agreement
7. From the language of constructive criticism to the language of deconstructive criticism

The first four chapters introduce you to mental languages and may seem the special province of those most interested in personal learning, while the next three chapters introduce you to social languages and may seem the special province of those most interested in leadership. We want to be clear at the outset that we intend a different message. On the contrary, this book can be read as an invitation to leaders—those charged with the responsibility to evaluate and often to help change the existing social arrangements—to consider the prior realm of internal change as crucial to their efforts and hopes.

The book can also be read as an invitation to those most interested in personal learning to consider that sustained learning of a transformational sort may require a social arrangement that supports it. The new technology you build in this book may provide a temporary thrust from, or perspective on, your own previously captivating equilibrium, but preserving this saving distance may require a new ongoing social arrangement, a "new language community" of some sort—keeping in mind that sometimes a community can be as small as two or three people, and that the ability to bring about new social arrangements is not reserved exclusively for leaders.

Having thus introduced seven new languages—four to transform customary mental arrangements and three to transform customary social arrangements; four to build a new technology, three to maintain it and upgrade it—the last two chapters speak to how we can deepen our practice of all seven languages and carry on the work that together we begin in this book.

Taken as a whole, the book intends to be a novel approach to the complex subject of why there is often so much of a slip between the cup of our own genuine aspirations for change—personally and collectively—and the lip of so little lasting change actually occurring. Although the ideas you find here are rooted in our own contemporary scholarship, theory building, and practice, our first identities are as teachers. In writing this book as teachers, we have taken inspiration from a Confucian text: "Tell me and I'll forget; show me and I may remember; but directly involve me, and I'll make it my own."

So, get ready. It's our plan to directly involve you, more than to present something to you. Welcome to the process of discovery that lies ahead; we hope you'll let us know the meaning you make of it.

The Internal Languages

Building the New Machine

Chapter One

From the Language of Complaint to the Language of Commitment

In the four chapters of Part One, we engage you directly in a creative process rooted in your own experience, to acquaint you intellectually with four languages for personal learning and reflective leadership. In particular, we intend to help you use the four languages to build the first-draft version of a custom-designed mental machine that enables you to overcome the gravitational pull of your own "third force," your own immunity to change.

The recurring rhythm of the first four chapters is as follows. We pose a question to you and ask you to think about it individually for a few minutes. We guide you in making notes about what comes up for you. We know that most of you are likely to work your way solo through this book, and that is fine. If you are able to work with a partner or partners, you have the added benefit of hearing these novel language forms out loud, and seeing more samples of what they produce than your own. Because we know that some readers are working with a partner and that some may be thinking of leading groups in this kind of learning, we want to take a moment before getting started to suggest a few ground rules we have found helpful.

Ground Rules for a Collaborative Experience in the First Four Chapters

If you can find one or two colleagues or friends to join you over the next four chapters, you'll likely value the help you get in building your own new technology and the chance to help others build theirs. If you are considering leading groups in this kind of learning, it may be helpful to know we have worked with groups as large as eight hundred and found the experience quite satisfying. Our only caution is that the "talk teams" stay a uniform two or three in size throughout the room, so that there is no large team whose members are always feeling "behind" in the developing process of inquiry, reflection, and checking in that occurs over these next four chapters.

Ground Rule for You as Speaker

Regarding these check-ins, as you'll see, the inquiries over these next four chapters get closer and closer to the bone. You may find you are happy to convey your reflections to others early on but prefer to let them in on less and less as things go further. This is why we suggest a main ground rule in your role as a speaker:

> How much or how little you want to let your partner
> (or partners) in on during these reflections
> is continuously *up to you and you alone.*

This includes, should you need to elect it, the perfectly acceptable and respectable choice to remain completely silent throughout, keeping all your thoughts to yourself.

Ground Rule for You as Listener

The ground rule in your role as a listener is this:

> It is not your job to point out to someone
> something you think he or she may be missing.

You do not have to give the supposed benefit of your own knowledge of the person's situation, or ask a question that intends to get the person to alter or reconsider that view, or in any other way teach the person anything. Rather, you are there to be a good listener, to allow others the opportunity to learn more about what they think when they have the liberty (too often amounting to the luxury) of speaking freshly made thoughts in public.

Ground Rule for You in Choosing a Talk Partner

To maximize this feeling of freedom, even with the first two ground rules, we advise you to be alert to another potential difficulty:

> It is preferable not to have talk partners with whom
> you have a subordinate or reporting relationship.

This also means you are not an optimal partner for one of *your* subordinates.

If you are able to arrange a talk-team (even a team of two) to travel together through these next four chapters, our recommendation is that you make your first pass through this material in a single sitting. We think you can do it in about an hour or two, depending on how long you want to check in with each other. Each chapter has its own point and purpose, but the four chapters in Part One taken together create a single mental machine and the means to run it. You are going to make use of it for the remainder of the book (and, hopefully, beyond). Of course, if you are traveling solo, you are creating this same technology yourself, so have no fear. In any case, because you are going to be gradually building your own unique conceptual map, you will need paper and pencil for the next four chapters to keep track of your work.

Activating the Internal Languages

Ready? Let's now pose the first question to you and give you a few minutes to ponder it individually. Write your thoughts on a separate sheet of paper for further reference.

What sorts of things—if they were to happen more frequently in your work setting—would you experience as being more supportive of your own ongoing development at work?

Before you get going on this question, a few elaborations:

1. We intend no special or highly technical meaning for *development* here; you should feel free to think about what would be

supportive to your own ongoing growth or development, however you wish to define it.

2. Don't edit your responses through a filter of reasonableness, possibility, or likelihood. We don't care if what occurs to you are things that you think have no chance of happening in your workplace. The question is just meant to create a thinking exercise. We're interested in whatever comes up for you, however likely or unlikely it is of being realized.

3. If you find it helpful, you may also (or instead) want to consider what sorts of troubling, diminishing, or constraining things—if they were to happen less frequently—you would also find more supportive of your development.

Also before you begin: once you've had a few minutes to actually think with a pen in your hand about this question, check in with your partner or partners about what you've come up with if you are doing this together, to the extent you wish to do so. Then, after you've had the time you need to check in, we invite you to read on. OK: take some time now for the question.

Of course, we have no way of knowing what particular thoughts occur to you as you ponder this question. But from having asked an enormous number of people from a great variety of professions to address this very question, we do have some hunches about what the tone or general nature of your conversation sounds like. This, by the way, is one of the reasons we do encourage you to move through these next four chapters conversationally, that is, with at least one other person. Each question we pose for you, when discussed with another, automatically generates a qualitatively different "language form." You will end up having a little direct, personal experience of each of the language forms we discuss in these chapters.

What have we found these conversations in response to our first question generally sound like? Here are some representative excerpts.

We *never* have a chance to really talk with each other about the bigger issues and questions surrounding our work. We're under so much pressure to deliver what is needed today or tomorrow that no one feels we can really afford to take the time out to think about the bigger picture. I know I need that, but I don't get it.

Well, let's see. My boss could die, move, or get promoted to another department! That would be a big support to my growth and development! (Laughter) Honestly, I don't see how I can grow that much, as long as she's in the picture. I don't respect her. She lies constantly. She thinks only about herself. I need to be able to respect my boss in order to grow. I need to have a partner or a team I really want to join with in order to grow. I don't have that.

To tell you the truth, what I need is one or two "me's" working for me the way I'm working for my boss. That would be the biggest support to my development. My area of responsibility has grown too large for me to handle by myself, and yet I can see there are other things I'd like to take on, but how can I? I need an associate or two to spread all this out and lighten the load.

Nobody really talks *to* each other in our shop; people talk *about* each other. There's an incredible amount of dysfunctional behind-the-back gossip, really, and running each other down. People have issues with other people, but the way we all handle it is that we talk about it with *other* people. We don't go to the person we have the issue with.

I'd be more able to grow and develop if I didn't have to be Mommy around here so much, if my subordinates didn't have to come to me for every little decision, would grow up and take more initiative and responsibility in their areas, so I was freer to do the same in my own.

If I had more time. It all comes down to that.

I can never tell my boss what I'm really thinking, and that's an obvious barrier to my growth. He just has this style of having it all together all the time, and of expecting everyone else to have it all together.

I feel like we go round and round addressing the same problems at work and never really solving them. We go on retreats. We dream big dreams. But real life goes on as it always has. Nothing really changes. It's hard to grow in an atmosphere like this.

The governance structure, power issues, the way decisions get made around here—all that is really screwed up. The wrong people are in charge. Even strategically, it's ineffective to make decisions concerning other people, not have them in on the decision, and then expect them to get behind the decision. C'mon! It's hard to grow in a place where you often feel you're being treated like a child.

The Default Mode: "NBC" and "BMW"

Nearly always, our first question elicits a language form that is actually highly familiar, and it astonishes us how easily, how protractedly, and how energetically people can produce it. It is a language that has a theme running through it—in whole or in part—of complaint, disappointment, or criticism. As one professional said to us

She: Oh, we're very good at this kind of talk where I work. We even have a name for it. We call it "NBC talk."

We: NBC talk? What's that?

She: NBC. Nagging, bitching, and complaining!

In another organization, they call it "BMW": bitching, moaning, whining.

In the movie *A Thousand Clowns,* the main character, Murray, says he's discovered that if you go up to people randomly at work or even on the street and tell them, "I'm sorry," they invariably respond in a way that suggests they do in fact carry around a storehouse of injured feelings about which they are subconsciously waiting for someone to apologize. We don't know if this is true. But we've made a similar discovery about another easily tapped storehouse. Ask people how they could be more supported at work, and a torrent of rueful criticism is released, sometimes accompanied by wan wishing and hoping: "If only . . ."; "I just wish . . ."; "If this once . . ."; "Why can't we (or he, or she) . . . ?"

Sometimes this kind of talk is filled with head-shaking amusement, sometimes resentment, sometimes weariness. It is a conversation produced by people who love their jobs, hate their jobs, feel mixed about their jobs; by people who are very good at their jobs, and not so good; by people who are new to work, and others near retirement. The criticisms are levied at bosses, subordinates, peers, "all of us"—and occasionally, even oneself.

The particular content of your own thoughts may or may not be anything like the examples we've given you. But whatever the content, it turns out we have a sharp eye and a good memory for an accumulation of ways we experience work as obstructing our own growth and development, and most of us have a well-practiced—and gloriously unproductive—way of dealing with this: we complain.

This conversation of what we can't stand is so pandemic in many work settings that it almost becomes second-nature and unnoticed. During a break at a recent workshop with middle managers, one of the participants came up to tell us how right we were about all the complaining that goes on in his shop. "I've got a joke for you, " he said, "which can help you make your point: What's the difference between your dog and your direct reports?" "All right," we said, a little reluctantly, noticing the group of eavesdropping fellow managers who had come nearer to hear the punch line. "What's the difference?" "The difference," he said, "is that when you let your dog into your office, it *stops* whining." While his fellow managers chuckled and nodded their heads, we couldn't help noticing that the joke, ostensibly at the expense of whiny subordinates, was itself a way of whining. This language form is widespread, but it may be easier to notice in others than in ourselves.

For those who do notice, its dominance can feel oppressive. As one professional told us:

> In our shop we have a group of very talented, very bright, and very funny people who have been here a long time, and they have polished the language of *kvetching* to a high art. They're very clever, very good at putting everything down. It becomes contagious; we all join in. And I have to admit, it *is* entertaining—in the way that a David Letterman or Howard Stern can be entertaining, in very small doses. But as the main staple of conversation, it's tremendously dispiriting and depressing because in the end the underlying message is a very discouraging, very cynical one: that everything is screwed up, and that there's really no possibility that anything can change for the better.

The language of complaining, wishing, and hoping is a highly frequented conversational form, but it is assuredly not one of our seven languages for personal learning and reflective leadership. Unlike our seven, it is not a relatively rare flower requiring a discourse-shaping language leader to carefully cultivate and nurture it. On the contrary, complaining grows on its own—and it grows everywhere, just like a weed. It is alive and well in nearly every work setting we've had anything to do with, whether high-functioning or underperforming.

The biggest problem with this NBC talk is precisely that it *doesn't* transform anything. It almost never goes anywhere; it becomes an end in itself. Complaining and wishing has its tiny virtues: it can allow people to let off steam; people can feel less alone in their disappointment, unhappiness, or resentment if they can find allies who share their negative characterization of something or someone. (Very often, it is a someone. "I think she's a jerk; do you think she's a jerk? Good, we both think she's a jerk!") But it rarely accomplishes much more than this.

The Potential in Complaint

So, why do we take your time to remind you of a widespread, non-transformational form of talk at work? We do so because we actually believe it is important to *pay attention to complaints* in a way people rarely do. We believe there is untapped potential here. Nontransformational though it might be, NBC talk contains the seed of a whole different language form. So widespread a manner of speaking demands our attention in part because it is so widespread, but also because it is so passionate. Where there is passion, there are also possibilities for transformation. We believe the language of complaint can be revisited for the purpose of being redeemed—that it contains a transformative element or seed. The route to that seed is found in this idea: *we would not complain about anything if we did not care about something.* Beneath the surface torrent of our complaining lies a hidden river of our caring, that which we most prize or to which we are most committed.

Far from thinking we need to turn our backs on the language of complaint (it is almost never a good idea to turn our backs on something in which people are investing so much energy), our perhaps peculiar-sounding message here is that leaders should consider fostering language contexts that *encourage* people to stay with, honor, and pursue further the transformative potential of their very complaints or disappointments.

The First Language: From Complaint to Commitment

How might we do this? We'd like to invite you not to lay aside but to revisit whatever you find yourself thinking about in response to our first question. To place you in a transformative relation to these thoughts or feelings, we ask you to consider a second question:

> What commitments or convictions that you hold are actually implied in your earlier response?

We imagine, if you take the time, that you can probably generate a number of commitments or convictions that are implicit in your reactions to our first question about what would support your development at work. But for our purposes at the moment, it is enough to pick just one you feel strongly about (or most strongly, if several come to mind). The quickest way of responding to this second question is just to complete the following sentence as you consider what you were thinking about in response to our first question:

> I am committed to the value or the importance of . . .

In these first four chapters, while we acquaint you with a number of relatively rare (but sustainable) language forms we introduce you to the activity of building a custom-designed mental machine—as we said in the Introduction, your own version of a new technology for personal learning, built to give you sufficient thrust or lift from your own captivating dynamic equilibrium. Each of the languages you meet in this and the next three chapters helps you create a piece of this machine. To keep track of its construction as you gradually build each piece, we suggest that you create on a separate piece of paper a four-column grid of the sort we provide in Figure 1.1.

Title the first column "Commitment" and enter the sentence stem as it appears in Figure 1.2.

Figure 1.1. Four-Column Conceptual Grid.

Column 1	Column 2	Column 3	Column 4

Figure 1.2. Column One Header.

1 Commitment	2	3	4
I am committed to the value or the importance of . . .			

Now enter your completion of the sentence stem "I am committed to the value or the importance of. . . ." If you are working with a partner or partners, we suggest you take the time to let each other in on what you come up with—to the extent you wish—before you read on.

Just to offer you a few examples, and to give us some common reference points, here is what the beginnings of three such maps of the mental machine might look like. The person who, earlier, made the following statement might have in column one what we see in Figure 1.3:

> Nobody really talks *to* each other in our shop; people talk *about* each other. There's an incredible amount of dysfunctional behind-the-back gossip, really, and running each other down. People have issues with other people, but the way we all handle it is that we talk about it with *other* people. We don't go to the person we have the issue with.

The person who said the following might enter in column one of his map what we show in Figure 1.4.

> I'd be more able to grow and develop if I didn't have to be Mommy around here so much; if my subordinates didn't have to come to me for every little decision, would grow up and take more initiative and responsibility in their areas, so I was freer to do the same in my own.

As a final example, the person who said the following might have entered in column one what we read in Figure 1.5.

> To tell you the truth, what I need is one or two "me's" working for me the way I'm working for my boss. That would be the biggest support to my development. My area of responsibility has grown too large for me to handle by myself, and yet I can see there are other things I'd like to take on, but how can I? I need an associate or two to spread all this out and lighten the load.

Figure 1.3. First Sample Map: Column One Complete.

1 Commitment	2	3	4
I am committed to the value or the importance of . . . *More open and direct communication at work.*			

Figure 1.4. Second Sample Map: Column One Complete.

1 Commitment	2	3	4
I am committed to the value or the importance of . . . *Supporting my staff to exercise more individual initiative.*			

Figure 1.5. Third Sample Map: Column One Complete.

1 Commitment	2	3	4
I am committed to the value or the importance of . . . *Securing sufficient resources and additional personnel support to thrive (rather than barely survive) in my job.*			

Presumably, no matter what you have in your first column, there are at least two things that can be said about it:

1. It represents a commitment you do genuinely hold (not one you feel you *should* hold, or one day aspire to hold, but genuinely do hold now).
2. It represents a commitment that is not, at the moment, fully or optimally realized (this should be true since, after all, we derived it from a prior language of deficit).

The Language of Our Commitments

In your first column, you are looking at a tiny instance of what we mean by the language of our commitments. Notice the path we have just walked and the nature of the shift we have just made, from the world of complaint to the world of commitment. We did not turn our backs on our complaints; on the contrary, we turn directly to them and pass through them to reach a world of commitment on the other side. The world of complaint is a highly populated and unproductive one at work, but rather than seeing it as a problem to be solved, a block to be dissolved, a virus to be killed, we invite leaders to make use of the energy available here by seeing it as a gateway to the less-populated and far more productive world of identifying and giving voice to our personal commitments at work. We build this gateway by fostering a language context—a place and disposition to honor our critical evaluations as opportunities to identify not only what we cannot stand but also the commitments we are ready to stand for.

Consider, for example, our usual range of responses, as leaders of anything, when people come to us with their complaints and criticisms about their circumstances at work. For most leaders, the range is limited to some or all of these responses:

1. We sympathize, empathize, and let the other know we see and understand how difficult he (or she or that) is.
2. Because our leadership position often affords us more information or a better vantage point on the circumstances at hand,

we may try to get the other to broaden her perspective, or consider additional elements of the situation.

3. Out of a generous, but sometimes misguided, impulse to be a bountifully providing leader who can heal the sick, fix the broken, and make all bad things go away, we may try to alter the world so that the reason for the initial complaint or criticism disappears.

We are not saying there is anything wrong with responses of this kind. Under various circumstances, each may be appropriate. We theorize, however, that we are more effective the wider our range of enactable responses to draw upon. As a corollary, it seems clear that the options we are unaware of are the ones we are least likely to elect. We believe there is a benefit to considering, as an additional possibility, a qualitatively different kind of response to complaining that brings about the language of our personal commitments. Let's see what this alternative response offers.

The Leadership Opportunity in the First Language

Our suggested alternative does not supply a verdict on the merits or demerits of the complaint. It does not merely take up neighborly residence within the complaint. It does not try to make the complaint go away by getting the person to change her mind, or by making the reason for the complaint disappear. Nor does it suggest there is anything unwelcome, disagreeable, or shameful about having a complaint. On the contrary, our alternative goes with the complaint, honors it, and invites the complaining person to follow the forward momentum that is implicit in the complaint.

We can do this by creating an opportunity for people to identify what they care most about in the situation at hand, to take some time to name what the most important issue or principle is at stake, and finally to identify what their complaint shows them they are most committed to. (Practically speaking, depending upon how angry or upset complaining people are, they may first need from us a sense that we do in fact understand—not necessarily agree with, but understand—what they are complaining

From the Language of
Complaint to the Language of Commitment.

Language of Complaint	Language of Commitment
• Easily and reflexively produced, widespread	• Relatively rare unless explicitly intended
• Explicitly expresses what we can't stand	• Explicitly expresses what we stand for
• Leaves the speaker feeling like a whiny or cynical person	• Leaves the speaker feeling like a person filled with conviction and hope
• Generates frustration and impotence	• Generates vitalizing energy
• Sees complaint as a signal of what's wrong	• Sees complaint as a signal of what someone cares about
• Nontransformational, rarely goes anywhere beyond letting off steam and winning allies to negative characterizations	• Transformational; anchors principle-oriented, purpose-directed work

about. They may be unable to accept our invitations until this need is met.) With such a response, complaining persons have the enabling opportunity to experience themselves more as committed persons than as complainers.

But the biggest beneficiary of this shift may be leaders themselves. Most leaders, for perfectly understandable reasons, do their best to avoid even finding out how large the language of complaint actually is in the sphere of their responsibility, or pursuing the depths of its particulars. Those who do find out, whether by plan or because it is unavoidably thrust in front of them, usually respond to the language of complaining as a tumor that must be shrunk. But people only complain about something because they are committed to the value or importance of something else. Thus in avoiding the energy and language of complaint, or regarding it as a force that needs to be expunged, we are also losing the chance to bring the vitalizing energy of commitment into the workplace.

As we are about to see in the chapter ahead, even though there is little that follows from complaining, a variety of developments are possible for us if we transform our complaints into the commitments that are the reason we even have our complaints in the first place.

If it is useful for us to consider inviting our subordinates into a new relationship to their complaints, it may be just as valuable for us to consider how we relate to our own ongoing language of dissatisfaction. Our mind is a little like a radio, continuously tuning in to various channels. Usually without realizing it, we channel surf from one ongoing program to another. We call this "the thinking we are doing," but since we are not really paying attention to our channel selection we are not so much thinking as "being thought." We don't really have these thoughts; *they have us.* There's the All Sports channel, the All News channel, and the All Complaining channel.

We care as much in this book about the language forms available to us when we are speaking to ourselves as when we are speaking with others. What is our usual relation to the familiar channel that internally signals our complaints, disappointments, and annoyances? Usually, we swing between fixing upon this channel (becoming preoccupied with our complaints and creating elaborate narratives about their origins, costs, and consequences—rich dramas in which we usually cast ourselves at the center as well-intentioned, beleaguered victim-heroes) and trying to ignore the channel (telling ourselves to stay positive, and not get bogged down in all this unproductive negativity). Interestingly, this second, supposedly mature position has as many risks in it as the first, since it involves not listening to ourselves—and ignoring our own internal instruments, which are sending us valuable information.

The language of our personal commitments suggests a third alternative to the usual seesawing between becoming preoccupied with what we can't stand on the one hand and ignoring our own complaints on the other. Practiced personally, the language of our personal commitments invites us to respect and honor our own complaints (rather than seeing them as something shameful, bothersome, or threatening). Through the exercise of the first language, we can actively turn toward them, regard them as a doorway to our deeper commitments, and walk into a room of wider possibility.

The language of complaint essentially tells us, and others, what it is we can't stand. The language of commitment tells us (and possibly others) what it is we stand for. Without having our complaints taken away and without giving them up, this first transforming language enables us to make a shift from experiencing ourselves as primarily disappointed, complaining, wishing, critical people to experiencing ourselves as committed people who hold particular convictions about what is most valuable, most precious, and most deserving of being promoted or defended. In Chapter Two, we turn to what follows from the ongoing experience of this new transforming language.

From the Language of Blame to the Language of Personal Responsibility

Let's take another look at what you have entered in the first column of your conceptual map: your own personal commitment. As we said in Chapter One, among other things this is a commitment that is not yet completely or optimally realized.

The Default Mode: We Have Met the Enemy and It Isn't Us!

Since we live in complex worlds, there are always many players and conditions that contribute to things being as they are. As a result, we can point to a variety of people and factors when we think about who or what is responsible for our commitments being less than fully realized.

Now, here's a question for you. If you put together a quick list of the people you see as responsible for your commitment not being fully realized, would your own name appear? This leads us to our next reflective question, the answer to which we invite you to enter in the second column of your conceptual map.

What are you doing, or not doing, that is keeping your commitment from being more fully realized?

Again, a few points before we turn you loose on this question.

First, we are not suggesting that you are the party who necessarily bears the greatest responsibility for your commitment not being fully realized. You may have only a little to do with it. We are certainly not saying, "It's all your fault!" We only suggest that there are very few situations in our adult lives where we do not have at least some hand in things being as they are. This is your chance to focus on your role, no matter how big or small a piece of the action it may be.

Similarly, we do not assume you are doing little or nothing on behalf of realizing your commitment. On the contrary, we assume that since you are giving your time to a book like this one, very likely you are the sort of person who is doing quite a lot to further your commitment. So let's agree you are doing quite a lot, but that this is not what we are asking you about. We are asking if you can identify anything you are doing that is also—perhaps quite inadvertently—keeping your commitment from being fully realized. We are also asking if you can identify anything you are *not* doing that is keeping your commitment from being fully realized.

An example of what we may do that keeps our commitment from being more fully realized is, "I agree to take on too many of the things I'm asked to do, and as a result I never have enough time to devote to what I'm really committed to." A common example of what we may *not* do that keeps our commitment from being more fully realized might be, "I'm not actually asking anyone for what I want," or "I'm not advocating forcefully enough for what I believe."

Think about your own contribution. Then enter what you've come up with in column two of the map that you began in Chapter One. You can head column two "What I'm Doing or Not Doing That Prevents My Commitment from Being Fully Realized" (see Figure 2.1). If you're doing this with a partner, take a moment to reflect and then check in to the extent you wish to do so.

$$\bigcirc$$

The Second Language:
From Blaming Others to Personal Responsibility

What is the language this question points us to? Let's drop in on what it sounds like to work with a large group of professionals who are at this same point you are at now in building the conceptual

Figure 2.1. Personal Responsibility.

1 Commitment	2 What I'm Doing or Not Doing That Prevents My Commitment from Being Fully Realized	3	4
I am committed to the value or the importance of . . .			

map. What we hear is the buzz of forty pairs of people in conversation about their second-column entries.

Lisa: OK, do any pairs *desperately* need more time to talk with each other about their column-two behaviors? (Laughter) I mean, you'll be back in your pairs in a moment. OK, OK, take another minute or so, and then we'll interrupt you. . . .

Lisa: OK, let's take a look at our four-column map here. Pat told us what was in her first column, her commitment. Now of course, she didn't *know*, when she told us what was in her first column (laughter), that she was going to have to spill her guts in front of the whole group for the rest of the afternoon! (Laughter) And, in fact, she does not *have* to. We always ask people if they want to pass or play on (laughter), and we mean it. It's perfectly fine at this point, or any future point, just to say you'd like to pass, and we'll move right along to the next person. So let's check with Pat. Pat, do you want to pass or play?

Pat: Oh, I'll play, what the heck! (Laughter and applause)

Lisa: OK, great. So, just in case everyone can't see the board, Pat said her first-column commitment was to the importance of valuing our employees, seeing them primarily as precious assets, something to protect and invest in, rather than as costs, something to contain or make less expensive. Now, what did you come up with in column two?

Pat: First of all, I realized, as I thought more about this, that this is a commitment to have our leadership team in particular regard our employees this way, especially my CEO. I believe that my CEO is not open to, or even the kind of person who might understand, what I was talking about if I described things this way. So I've let that keep me from even approaching him about this. To be honest, I've never explicitly laid out my vision to him.

Lisa: Thank you. Did you hear what Pat just did there? Maybe I will take a moment to tell you, at least, what I heard. First, she got a little clearer about what her commitment really meant, and she launched into a characterization of the CEO as responsible for the way employees are valued—which might even be totally accurate. That is, she started with a little *kvetching* (laughter), the old familiar language of what she can't stand—but she didn't stop there. Our invitation was for Pat to consider *her* responsibility for her commitment not being fully realized. And she got there. She's saying—if I get it—that she's holding, without having really tested it, a discouraging impression of her CEO. To put it simply, she has not explicitly talked with the boss about her vision. And we're sure that when it comes to not talking with someone who may be key to things changing in the direction we'd like, Pat is probably the *only* person in this whole room who has ever clammed up like this, right? (Laughter) OK, we're not saying we are all identical, and that everyone would sign onto every single thing people could tell us about their second column; but we are saying there is probably *nothing* someone could say about what's in their second column that there wouldn't be someone else in the room who could also say "amen" to it. Thank you, Pat. Now let's turn to Michael. Michael, do you want to pass or play on?

You can see, from this "audio clip," that we use the public occasion of the group to create a little direct experience of the second language at work. In a friendly, uncoerced, and laughing-at-ourselves way, we invite the room to fill up with the language of personal responsibility, declarations of our unproductive action and inaction. We tell stories on ourselves, not for the purpose of humiliating or diminishing ourselves but to begin putting them in a place where we can look at them and learn from them. We tell our stories so we can stop *being* our stories and become persons who *have* these stories. We tell these stories so that we can become more responsible for them.

Why? We have probably all had the experience of being in a conversation or confrontation with someone who is upset with us about something. Perhaps they are cataloging a litany of our faults or misdeeds. We find ourselves thinking, *I wouldn't say I'm innocent of every offense you charge me with. I'd even be willing to say that you are more right than wrong about my piece of this problem. But, my goodness! I just wish you were one-tenth as perceptive about your own responsibility in this situation as you are about my responsibility!* We are not asking to be let off the hook. We are just asking the other person to put herself on the hook, too, so we can swing together instead of swinging away.

Hopefully, we have all also had the rarer experience of being in a confrontational conversation with someone whom we did feel was consistently taking responsibility for her own piece of the problem at the same time she was taking us to task. Perhaps we have experienced how much further we can go with the other when the other is also taking responsibility for his end. Leaders who take an interest in fostering the language of personal responsibility are likely to find themselves in far more productive conversations with their employees and are likely to foster far more productive conversations among their employees. But just as important, as we are about to see, the practice of this language form increases the possibility that we can engage in much more productive conversations with *ourselves*.

Presumably, if you are joining in by creating your own conceptual map, you have now made notes in your second column that suggest a "story" you can tell on yourself. Let's check back with some of those conceptual maps-in-the-making that were started in the previous chapter. The person who, earlier, made the following statement might now have a conceptual map that looks like the one in Figure 2.2.

Nobody really talks *to* each other in our shop; people talk *about* each other. There's an incredible amount of dysfunctional behind-the-back gossip, really, and running each other down. People have issues with other people, but the way we all handle it is that we talk about it with *other* people. We don't go to the person we have the issue with.

The person who said the following might now have a map that looks like Figure 2.3.

I'd be more able to grow and develop if I didn't have to be Mommy around here so much, if my subordinates didn't have to come to me for every little decision, would grow up and take more initiative and responsibility in their areas, so I was freer to do the same in my own.

Figure 2.2. First Example of a Two-Column Version of the Map.

1 Commitment	2 What I'm Doing or Not Doing That Prevents My Commitment from Being Fully Realized	3	4
I am committed to the value or the importance of . . . *More open and direct communication at work.*	*I don't speak up when people are violating the norm I value. Silently, I collude in it being OK to talk behind one another's back.*		

Figure 2.3. Second Example of a Two-Column Version of the Map.

1 Commitment	2 What I'm Doing or Not Doing That Prevents My Commitment from Being Fully Realized	3	4
I am committed to the value or the importance of . . . *Supporting my staff to exercise more individual initiative.*	*(1) When they ask me to get involved or take over, I don't refuse.* *(2) I don't delegate as much as I could.* *(3) I too often am willing to be drawn into things when I should refer to the subordinate who is in charge of that area.*		

Finally, the person who said the following might now have a map that looks like the one in Figure 2.4.

> To tell you the truth, what I need is one or two "me's" working for me the way I'm working for my boss. That would be the biggest support to my development. My area of responsibility has grown too large for me to handle by myself, and yet I can see there are other things I'd like to take on, but how can I? I need an associate or two to spread all this out and lighten the load.

The little notes or sentence fragments appearing in column two stand for a story or stories we tell on ourselves. The act of telling them is a form of responsibility, acknowledging our own hand in things being less than we hope, less than we intend, less than we are committed to their being. When do we normally have opportunities to tell such stories, and what is our accustomed course of action when we do?

Obscuring the Potential in Self-Responsibility

The language of personal responsibility is another relatively rare form of sustained speech at work. It does sometimes appear—in a tiny, distorted, and short-lived form—on the occasion of year-end reviews. Perhaps we are asked to assess our accomplishments and shortcomings in the work year now drawing to a close. Maybe we sit with our boss and, after considering our successes or personal strengths, turn to a highly atrophied version of the language of personal responsibility by owning up to our failures or limitations (or the ever-popular "growing edge"). Why is such conversation so pale a version of what we are talking about here?

Look at the usual outcome of owning up to our limitations and shortcomings in a year-end review. Such conversations lead to the work equivalent of New Year's Resolutions. They have about the same transformative power of New Year's Resolutions, which, as we all know, is rather puny: by March we are no longer keeping the resolution, and by May we have forgotten what it was.

A New Year's Resolution approach to the actions and inactions that prevent our own commitments from being more fully realized essentially frames the behaviors we list in our second column as

Figure 2.4. Third Example of a Two-Column Version of the Map.

1 Commitment	2 What I'm Doing or Not Doing That Prevents My Commitment from Being Fully Realized	3	4
I am committed to the value or the importance of . . . *Securing sufficient resources and additional personnel support to thrive (rather than barely survive) in my job.*	*I don't or can't say NO!*		

expressions of professional misbehavior or ineffectiveness. We thus frame such behaviors as the work equivalent of naughtiness. By contrast, in this book we suggest that taking responsibility goes well beyond taking the blame.

It also goes beyond making things right, or cleaning up one's act, admirable though such intentions might be. After all, in many cases, we don't even need the presence of the boss or a year-end review to make us resolve to do better. We do it all on our own. What, for example, is the first reaction of conscientious professionals to identifying a way in which their actions or inactions are undermining their own commitments? They immediately write on their characterological to-do list to clean up their act and set things right (or at least "righter").

Asking people to fill in the second column, we have seen on many occasions that they write: "I've got to start saying *no*" or "I have to delegate more often and more consistently." In other words, they let the story of how they are undermining their own commitments live for about two seconds, and then they immediately set to work to quote-unquote correct their error or solve their problem. What could possibly be the matter with this? Surely it's what any employer would want, a kind of personal responsibility to identify the bugs in the system and debug it.

But strange as it may sound, even though something is surely gained when a problem is solved, something is also lost. For one thing, we lose the problem. "But that's the point!" the conscientious professional responds. "What could be wrong with having one less problem?" Our reply is that, without doubt, many problems may need only to be solved, but if we regard all our problems as bugs in the system, the best we will ever do in removing them is preserve the system—and it may be responsible for producing the bugs in the first place! When we solve a problem quickly, the one thing we can usually be certain of is that we ourselves are the same people coming out of the problem as we were going into it.

A Curricular Approach to Personal Responsibility

Although it will take us another chapter or two to be fully clear about what we mean by taking responsibility, for us it involves more than taking the blame or debugging the system. It involves being able to learn from the behaviors we identify, to learn from the story we tell on ourselves. If some of our problems are actually lessons, are actually stories to learn from, then in solving problems of this kind too quickly we risk losing the lesson or making the moral of the story disappear. We would be better off, it turns out, *not* solving some problems, but instead sticking with them in hopes they can "solve us." What does this mean?

The problems that solve us are those from which we genuinely learn. They change how we think. These are what we call good problems, the ones we are wise not to pass through too quickly. What, for example, does a teacher have in mind when she assigns her pupils a set of math problems to work on overnight? How much does she really care about the solutions? Has she sent them off like workers in some cottage industry, eagerly waiting for her little charges to return with their homespun solutions that she now intends to sell like handcrafted weavings?

The point of the problem is not really that the students produce solutions. In fact, if the students too easily solve the problems, the teacher does not even regard them as good problems. The idea is not so much that the learners solve the problems as that the problems solve the learners. The good problems require the students to stretch and change their own math understanding. Good teachers bother their students in useful ways. They give them problems for their own good. This collection of good problems for our learning is what is meant by a curriculum.

For our learning as adults, we are no less in need of a rich curriculum, a collection of good problems with which we can bear hanging out. But no clever educator need write our curriculum. It is waiting there in the text and tangle of our everyday experience, waiting to be formed out of the very behaviors we have just identified: the apparent *mis*behavior of keeping our commitments from being fully realized.

**From the Language of Blame to
the Language of Personal Responsibility.**

Language of Blame	Language of Personal Responsibility
• Easily and reflexively produced and widespread; comfortable to express	• Relatively rare, in an ongoing way, unless explicitly intended; uncomfortable to express
• Holds the other person responsible for gaps between committed intentions and reality	• Expresses specific behaviors we personally engage in and fail to engage in that contribute to gaps
• Frequently generates frustration, alienation, and impotence in speaker	• Draws on the momentum of our commitments
• Frequently generates defensiveness in others	• Frequently generates productive conversation about both parties' contributions to gap
• Nontransformational; rarely goes anywhere; deflects our attention to places where we have little or no direct influence	• Transformational; directs our attention to places where we have maximum influence
• At best, raises questions only for others	• Raises questions for oneself

In Chapter One, we asked you not to set aside your complaints, disappointments, and criticism but to honor them by staying with them, taking them deeper, and transforming them into the language of your commitments. In a similar way, we now invite you to stay with (rather than too quickly resolve to fix) your undermining behaviors, in order to take them deeper and let them carry you to a transformative (rather than merely *corrective*) position. In the end, the reason New Year's Resolutions to correct professional misbehavior have so little power is that in treating such behavior as the work equivalent of naughtiness, we are ultimately being disrespectful of our own complexity. We are ignoring the powerful source of these behaviors, behaviors that will never change without somehow directly addressing their source.

What language form would assist us in honoring, and being more fully responsible for, that complexity? What language can help us create, out of this same misbehavior, the stuff of good problems we can learn from? To answer these questions, in Chapter Three we turn to the third column in our conceptual map.

From the Language of New Year's Resolutions to the Language of Competing Commitments

Diagnosing the Immunity to Change

Why does merely resolving to eliminate our undermining behavior, in column two of the conceptual map, tend to have so little effect? Why do even our sincerest intentions and New Year's Resolutions to clean up our acts have so little power? We have suggested an answer: that there may be bigger forces at work, behind the behaviors of column two, and if we don't get these forces onto the table they continue to run the show. What might these bigger forces be?

Activating the Potential of Self-Responsibility

Take a close look at what you have captured in your own second column (go back to your work in Chapter Two). Can you sense anything even vaguely like a fear or discomfort if you consider doing differently what you have indicated in column two?

Let's say you entered in that column:

I don't really take a stand with my boss for the time I need to complete my assignments to my satisfaction. I just keep handing off to him on his schedule without talking about how much better the work could be with a more realistic time frame.

Our question to you is, When you think of doing otherwise, are you aware of anything that feels even vaguely like a fear or worry? Perhaps you reply, "Well, I worry he'll think I'm not really up to the job." Or maybe there's a completely different kind of anxiety: "I worry he'll tell me he's perfectly happy with half-assed quality, that 'good enough' is good enough, and that's something I really don't want to find out."

Now, you may be thinking we're suggesting that the bigger power behind our column-two behavior is our fears. Actually, we're not. Although our fears often are hidden from our view—and it is true we rarely discuss our fears honestly or hear about others'—fear alone is not the bigger power we have in mind. It is, however, a valuable gateway to that bigger power.

If we just stop at this gateway, with our fears, we tend to relate to our undermining behaviors too passively. We say, "I have a fear of being out of control," or "not being well thought of," or "finding out that others do not hold the same standards of excellence that I do"—as if this were just a burdensome condition of our existence. "I have a fear of making others uncomfortable" is roughly equivalent to "I have a cold," or "I have a bad back." In other words, we are naming an unfortunate condition of our existence. "It's just something I'm stuck with," we're saying; "something that showed up, and something that just doesn't go away, just like a chronic cold or back condition. I'm carrying on with my commitments as best I can in spite of these burdens."

Something else happens if we relate to our fears more actively, by considering that we may not just *have* our fears: we discover we may be actively committed to keeping those things that we are afraid of from happening. It's one thing to say, "I'm afraid if I ask for it I'll be turned down," or "I'm afraid to discover my boss's standards are so low." It's quite another thing to say, "I may be actively committed to *not* putting myself in a situation where I can be disappointed" or "I may be committed to not learning what my boss's standards really are." With this alternative language, we enter a different world. We walk through the gateway. We take a step toward putting the bigger powers into play.

Behind the behaviors of column two, we suggest, are other commitments that we hold. Identifying these commitments can lead, as we will see, to a more encompassing field for our learning.

It is to these other commitments that we turn, as you might expect, in column three of the conceptual map of our mental machine. Once we do so, it is very hard to turn back to the old understanding of ourselves.

This next invitation brings us into a more three-dimensional world for self-reflection and is perhaps the most difficult conceptual leap in this book. It calls for a kind of let-the-chips-fall-where-they-may courage. But once we complete it, we have a whole new perspective on our own third force, the dynamic equilibrium that tends to keep things as they are.

The Third Language: From New Year's Resolutions to Competing Commitments

Here's how it works. Having identified the fear or discomfort associated with doing other than you are doing in column two, take this a step further by framing the fear (however odd this may at first sound) as an *active commitment of yours to keep the thing you are afraid of from happening*. This is what goes in column three of your conceptual map, headed "Competing Commitment" (Figure 3.1).

If my fear in advocating with my boss for the value of more time with my assignments is that he won't think I'm up to the job, then I might enter into column three: "I am or may be committed to not being seen by my boss as inadequate for the job." This is a perfectly reasonable commitment to hold (even if we don't often acknowledge we hold it). If the fear is more about learning that my boss doesn't really care at what level of quality the work is performed, I might write, "I am committed to not learning that my boss is willing to settle for mediocrity."

We know that these sound like odd commitments to hold, and that if you are like most people you seldom, if ever, consider thoughts and feelings such as these as commitments. Let us remind you that you are not required to buy any of these ideas; you're just renting them, for the time you spend with this book, to see if something new and useful appears for you as a result. Although we don't usually consider we hold commitments such as these, if we do they name not just something we are stuck with, like a cold or a bad back, but interestingly an active, energy-expending way of living. They name a way our creativity is being continuously

Figure 3.1. Competing Commitment.

1 Commitment	2 What I'm Doing or Not Doing That Prevents My Commitment from Being Fully Realized	3 Competing Commitment	4
I am committed to the value or the importance of . . . *Producing work to my own standards.*	*I don't really take a stand with my boss for the time I need to complete assignments to my satisfaction.*		

spent, and spending it this way may be a clue to how our own temporizing equilibrium—our own immune system—sustains itself.

The commitments of column one are the sort we would be proud to stand on a chair and proclaim to our professional colleagues. "We are genuinely committed," we say, "to more open communication," or "to a more inclusive, collaborative style of leadership," and we mean it. We are less likely to stand on some metaphorical chair and tell our professional community, "I am committed to having things done my way," or "to not learning things that it will be disappointing or discouraging for me to discover," or "to being loved and admired." Yet these things can *also* be true.

We (the authors) are not saying that now finally we are getting to the unseemly truth: that our first-column commitments are our fake, shiny-gloss, pretend commitments, and that our third-column commitments are the unvarnished truth of the matter. We believe you genuinely hold the commitments you name in your first column, just as we genuinely hold those that appear in our own first columns. But we also believe that adults are complex. We may compose a multitude of commitments and if we don't bring the different sorts before us, we are unlikely, in building our machine, to create something with sufficient power to alter our modes of operating. Our "reflecting" will amount to tinkering with what is only a piece of the action; our leadership, no matter how hard we work at it, will be on behalf of easily reversible changes that bring us back to the status quo.

Somewhere, earlier on, most of us have developed a sanitized, idealized conception of the masterful or high-performing professional as a person who checks at the door to work the clutter and distraction of the all-too-human third-column commitments. We imagine some person who only enters with the bright white cloak of first-column commitments. In this book we do not favor this way of distinguishing between more-able and less-able professionals. We believe it is impossible for anyone to leave behind her third-column commitments. "Wherever you go, there you are," the saying has it. *There we are,* with our first-column commitments; and there we are with our third-column commitments as well. The distinction we favor is between those who know they bring their third-column commitments with them and those who do not.

Before taking this discussion further, why don't we stop and give you a chance to generate your own third-column commitment? To recap:

1. Look at what you have in your second column (from your work in Chapter Two).
2. See if you can identify anything even vaguely like a fear or discomfort associated with doing other than what you have written in column two.
3. Enter this in your third column as a possible commitment you hold to *prevent* that thing which you are afraid of from happening.

As always, if you are doing this with a partner or partners we encourage you to take a moment and then check in with each other as to what you came up with.

A Checkpoint in Using the Third Language

Before we turn you loose on this, here is a tip to self-monitor whether you're on the right track. If you look at what comes up for you, or what you enter in the third column, and find yourself a little "creeped out" by what it says, if it bothers you a little, if you say to yourself, "Jeez, I dealt with this ten years ago in therapy, and now here it is again!" or, "I remember thinking about this once a few years ago, and I told myself I'd never think about it again"—these are all good signs! It shows you've held yourself to the reflective process.

If, on the other hand, you look at what you come up with and it has a distinctly noble ring to it ("I'm committed to my department doing as well as it can," or "I'm committed to more time with my children"), then this is a sign that you are somehow slipping off the rails. We don't doubt that such a commitment is genuine and describes something important about you. It's just that it does not allow you to build the most powerful mental machine possible for you. If you find that your new commitment does indeed have too noble a ring to it, we suggest you interrogate your new commitment a level further, vis-à-vis possible fears, anxieties, or discomforts; for example, "and if my department were not to be doing as well as it could, what fear would arise for me then?" Your commitment to avoiding this fear might then lead you to a productively disturbing result.

In essence, whatever we enter in the third column should have this common feature: it names a particular form of *self-protection* to which we are committed, and which competes with the commitment in our first column.

OK, now we invite you to fill in your third column. When you've completed it, you are ready to look at the maps of the three people we've been following in the first two chapters.

The first person, you'll remember, began this way:

Nobody really talks *to* each other in our shop; people talk *about* each other. There's an incredible amount of dysfunctional behind-the-back gossip, really, and running each other down. People have issues with other people, but the way we handle it is that we talk about it with *other* people. We don't go to the person we have the issue with.

This is what she said to her partner in the check-in after filling in her third column:

I think what I'd really be most afraid of in calling people on their backbiting and gossip is that people would see me as the Tough Woman, you know? The Activist, the Crusader. Deep down, this is probably who I really am, but I've seen what happens when you're tagged with this reputation, and I don't like it. Especially if you're a woman. I want people to be comfortable with me, and see me as part of the group. I don't really like being the odd person out.

Figure 3.2 is what her conceptual map now looks like.

The second person began this way:

I'd be more able to grow and develop if I didn't have to be Mommy around here so much, if my subordinates didn't have to come to me for every little decision, would grow up and take more initiative and responsibility in their areas, so I was freer to do the same in my own.

Figure 3.2. First Example of a Three-Column Version of the Map.

1 Commitment	2 What I'm Doing or Not Doing That Prevents My Commitment from Being Fully Realized	3 Competing Commitment	4
I am committed to the value or the importance of . . .		I may also be committed to . . .	
More open and direct communication at work.	*I don't speak up when people are violating the norm I value. Silently, I collude in it being OK to talk behind one another's back.*	*Not being seen as the Brave Crusader, Castrating Bitch, or Miss Holier-Than-Thou; . . . having people feel comfortable with me.*	

From this he generated the two columns that we saw in Figure 2.3 in Chapter Two. He describes his fears this way in acting differently from what he's indicated in column two:

> If I didn't step in when they asked me to, I'd be afraid they'd feel I was an abandoning leader and that they'd be very unhappy with me. If I were to delegate more, or refer more and not get drawn in, I'm afraid, to be honest, that the outcome or work product would suffer and things would not come off to my satisfaction.

In Figure 3.3 we see what his four-column conceptual map now looks like.

The third person began like this:

> To tell you the truth, what I need is one or two 'me's' working for me the way I'm working for my boss. That would be the biggest support to my development. My area of responsibility has grown too large for me to handle by myself, and yet I can see there are other things I'd like to take on, but how can I? I need an associate or two to spread all this out and lighten the load.

From this, she generated the two columns shown in Figure 2.4 in Chapter Two.

In considering her fears, her internal monologue was quick and to the point: "I absolutely hate all conflict with a passion. I would rather do anything than get into a fight, argument, or confrontation with someone over the age of twenty-one."

Her conceptual map now appears as we see it in Figure 3.4.

Presumably you now have something in your third column as well. Whatever it might be, one thing should be true: it names a particular form of self-protection, a particular kind of unhappiness that, whether you realize it or not, you especially want to avoid. If the first-column commitment names a kind of heaven we want to bring onto earth, then the third-column commitment is a little window into a kind of hell we are trying to keep from breaking out on earth! Like the idea in George Orwell's novel *Nineteen Eighty-Four*—that each person has her or his own custom-designed apprehension of hell—the third column should provide at least a glimpse into an aspect of yours.

Figure 3.3. Second Example of a Three-Column Version of the Map.

1 Commitment	2 What I'm Doing or Not Doing That Prevents My Commitment from Being Fully Realized	3 Competing Commitment	4
I am committed to the value or the importance of . . . *Supporting my staff to exercise more individual initiative.*	*(1) When they ask me to get involved or take over, I don't refuse.* *(2) I don't delegate as much as I could.* *(3) I too often am willing to be drawn into things when I should refer to the subordinate who is in charge of that area.*	**I may also be committed to . . .** *Not having my staff feel like I've abandoned them; not having my staff unhappy with me; not having our work product be less than I think I could do on my own, even if it means disempowering or failing to empower my staff.*	

Figure 3.4. Third Example of a Three-Column Version of the Map.

1 Commitment	2 What I'm Doing or Not Doing That Prevents My Commitment from Being Fully Realized	3 Competing Commitment	4
I am committed to the value or the importance of . . . *Securing sufficient resources and additional personnel support to thrive (rather than barely survive) in my job.*	*I don't or can't say NO!*	I may also be committed to . . . *Avoiding all conflict, at all costs.*	

Self-Cleansing Transformed to Commitment to Self-Reflection

Our third-column commitments name something of greater consequence than a disposition, trait, or attitude (such as "I don't like to make others feel threatened"); they name a way in which we may be actively spending ourselves ("I am committed to not making others feel threatened"). They tell us an important thing we are up to—doing—in our lives. They also remind us we are doing what we are doing on behalf of a powerful, normal, human motive: to protect ourselves. There need be nothing shameful about self-protection; in fact, in the abstract, self-protection is clearly a crucial act of self-respect.

The problem is not that we are self-protective, but that we are often unaware of being so. Without accepting responsibility for the forms our self-protection takes, we are inclined to view our second-column behaviors as signs of weakness and to resolve bravely to clean up our act and do better. Or we are inclined to look outside ourselves should the commitments for which we *do* accept responsibility—our first-column commitments—fail to realize the results we anticipated.

The Three Columns Create a Pathway: Our Own Immune System Comes into View

When read backwards, the three columns we have so far constructed constitute what in medicine would be called a "pathway," explicating a process of disease. Our third-column commitment (taking our third person as an example, "I'm committed to avoiding all conflict, at all costs") leads to certain behaviors ("I don't or can't say NO!") that in turn undermine our first-column commitment ("I'm committed to securing sufficient resources . . .").

Notice that in this interpretation our "symptoms," the second-column behaviors, take on a whole other character when viewed through the lens of the third column. Now they are not well understood merely as forms of professional misbehavior or ineffectiveness; they are instead perfectly consistent, faithful, effective, and even brilliant expressions of our third-column commitments! If I am actually committed to not being seen as Miss Holier-Than-Thou, then I absolutely should not speak up when others violate the norm I value. I should speak up even *less* than I already do! This is not a sign of my incompetence or a sloppy aspect of my professional performance; it's a brilliantly consistent and clearly effective expression of my commitment. It's exactly how I *should* behave! If I am committed to not having my staff feel abandoned, then I should *not* refuse to get drawn into things I could refer to subordinates. I should micromanage even more than I already do. If I'm committed to avoiding conflict, then not saying no is just exactly what I ought to be doing; I should refuse or decline even less!

People may never be effective in altering column-two behaviors, we are suggesting, unless they first recognize how the behaviors are effective, consistent expressions of a bigger purpose the person too rarely brings into conversation with others, or with oneself.

The only problem is that these consistent, effective, conscientious, and faithful behaviors also have the effect of undermining our admirable, genuinely held first-column commitments. The first column and the third column are inevitably in contradictory tension with each other; yet they are both true, and held simultaneously. How is this possible?

Oddly enough, and counterintuitive though it may seem, such contradictions are precisely what is required to maintain any mental system that has further room to grow. If the system is in some way limited, incomplete, partial, or distorted (this describes *any* mental system, short of one that is completely encompassing or fully evolved—an uncommon, hard-to-find end state in nature), such contradictions are the rule, not the exception. They are not only possible but necessary if the system is to remain in operation. A system that does not contain within itself perfect balance (and nearly none do) maintains its balance through countervailing forces, each of which alone would overturn the system in an opposite direction.

This living contradiction—these countervailing balances—compose what we call the third force, the process of dynamic equilibrium that works with breathtaking power and effectiveness to keep things pretty much as they are. This is an instance of our immune system, the way we continuously manufacture antigens to change. What the three people we have been following (and you, if you have been building your own machine as you read) have created is their (and your) custom version of such a dynamic equilibrium (see Figure 3.5).

Figure 3.5. The First Three Columns
as a Map of an Immune System.

1 Commitment	2 What I'm Doing or Not Doing That Prevents My Commitment from Being Fully Realized	3 Competing Commitment
I am committed to the value or the importance of . . .		I may also be committed to . . .
More open and direct communication at work.	I don't speak up when people are violating the norm I value. Silently, I collude in it being OK to talk behind one another's back.	Not being seen as the Brave Crusader, Castrating Bitch, or Miss Holier-Than-Thou; . . . having people feel comfortable with me.
Supporting my staff to exercise more individual initiative.	(1) When they ask me to get involved or take over, I don't refuse. (2) I don't delegate as much as I could. (3) I too often am willing to be drawn into things when I should refer to the subordinate who is in charge of that area.	Not having my staff feel like I've abandoned them; not having my staff unhappy with me; not having our work product be less than I think I could do on my own, even if it means disempowering or failing to empower my staff.
Securing sufficient resources and additional personnel support to thrive (rather than barely survive) in my job.	I don't or can't say NO!	Avoiding all conflict, at all costs.

No matter how genuinely I may be committed (like the third person in Figure 3.5) to securing the additional resources I need, I may also be committed to avoiding conflict at all cost, and my simultaneous living out of this commitment generates behaviors that undermine the first-column commitment. So long as this third commitment is a part of the picture (and we all have some similar kind of third-column commitment in our respective pictures), no amount of altering our second-column behaviors is likely to have a lasting effect.

The Third Force and Leading for Change

This may be easier to see on a larger, public canvas. Many of our professions have a history of trying to effect dramatic reforms in the institutions they shape. Many of us have participated in organizations seeking to advance new visions. In recent times, work settings have been genuinely, even heroically, trying to "reengineer," achieve "total quality," make the workplace "more inclusive" or "flatter"; they may be seeking to integrate the "new technologies," be more "customer-oriented," "plan for innovation," or respond to a variety of Myers-Briggs styles among the leaders. The word *reform* has become so attached to the words *school, health care,* and *court* that one has the impression the professions of education, medicine, and the judiciary are in continuous reconstruction. Today's business organizations, in or out of the new economy, are under nearly constant pressure to reorganize themselves to solve critical problems or take advantage of quickly disappearing windows of opportunity.

When any group achieves even a critical mass of like-minded participants dedicated to a common purpose such as some kind of change, what we see is a shared first-column commitment. A collectively owned first-column commitment is what we usually call a vision or mission. Effective leaders go to enormous lengths, as well they should, to create a viable mission, a shared commitment to which there is the widest possible assent. But when they do, they foster only one among several language forms that may be necessary for success. What happens if, having fostered a language for our public commitments, no language is fostered for our hidden ones?

In the world of primary and secondary education, for example, curricular designers and school reformers have been (though unrecognized) creating a narrative about change for much of this century. In various seasons, whole schools, school systems, or national reform movements crystallize a shared first-column commitment to bring about important changes in how our children are schooled. As anyone knows who has followed these well-intentioned waves of reform, there is nearly always, as we suggested in the Introduction, a lot of slip between the cup and the lip.

This is just as common a situation in the world of business. Visions are articulated, but nothing happens. Plans are created, and even beautifully published; yet they often end up sitting on a shelf somewhere. Companies even summon a collective intention to carry out the plans. Global corporations pay consulting firms millions of dollars for strategic plans that the corporate leadership feels are worth every penny. "The plans make brilliant sense," they say. "We should carry them out, and we will," they say. But they don't. Noble aspirations often lead to little change. The mighty mountain heaves and gives forth a mouse.

Why are the outcomes so frequently pale in relation to the vivid color of the aspirations? Why does so little real change actually occur? Why do the reformers so often reproduce something that looks too much like the original model?

There is no lack of answers to these questions, but the blame is usually assigned to other people or unanticipated obstacles:

They undermined us.

Resistance.

Expectations were too high, and people thought we could do too much, too quickly.

The population we were dealing with was too difficult.

We didn't have adequate resources.

There weren't enough of us.

A real reform takes ten years, and the average superintendent stays less than five.

In the end, top management lacked courage.

Any of these things could be true. But we suspect, as did Pogo ("I have found the enemy, and he is *us*!"), that a bigger piece of the problem may rest with the reformers themselves. No matter how hard and genuinely we may work on behalf of our first-column commitment (the vision, the public heaven we are trying to bring to earth), is it possible we are also working—and with more effective results—in service of a competing, third-column commitment (to self-protection, to a private hell we are trying to keep *away* from earth)?

There is a critical piece too often left out of the organizational change process. It rests on a simple premise with a single corollary. The premise: it may be nearly impossible for us to bring about any important change in a system or organization without changing ourselves (at least somewhat). The corollary is that for every commitment we genuinely hold to bring about some important change, there is another commitment we hold that has the effect of preventing the change. If the stories of organizational reform and change we continue to create are such partial stories, stories that only tell half the truth, we cannot expect to succeed.

If we say, "I haven't the time for all this soul-searching; let's just jump in, get into action, and we'll work out the problems as we come upon them," it's easy to predict that we will end up puzzled as to why such good intentions led to such disappointing results. The road to hell, we have long been told, is paved with good intentions. But we haven't had a good enough blueprint to understand how the road gets built this way.

The First Three Languages Together Create a Missing Map

What have the three languages, taken together, so far enabled us to make? A discouraging answer might be that we have managed to bring into view a picture of our own immune system, our own third force, our own contradiction-laden system operating to ensure we will be able to do little to realize our own genuine commitments for personal or organizational change. We may, for example, be genuinely committed to fostering a more collaborative form of leadership in the exercise of our authority, but we may also be committed to being in control, or having things go our way, or having the work product reach our standard. Serving the two commitments may actually have us working against ourselves.

How should we regard the circumstance of our being self-contradictory? An understandable reaction would be to regard this as a kind of problem, even an embarrassing one. We certainly don't tend to think of it as an asset. If you were asked by a prospective employer at the end of a job interview why he should hire you, you are not likely to say, "Because I'm well qualified, share the same goals as this company . . . and, oh, yes, I'm a bundle of contradictions!" We tend instead to see our self-contradictions as a problem. A conscientious response to identifying a problem, as we all know, is to get at solving it as quickly as possible. But quite a different stance toward our contradictions is possible, as Walt Whitman's words suggest: "Do I contradict myself? Very well, then. I contradict myself! I am vast! I contain multitudes!" What is true of Whitman is true of each of us as well. We are vast. We contain multitudes.

Why might a friendlier, welcoming stance toward our contradictions be in order? If you ask a developmental psychologist to stand on one leg (as Rabbi Hillel in the Hebrew Scriptures was asked) and explain as succinctly as possible what conditions contribute to a person's growth, the answer will probably be something like this: "An ingenious combination of support and challenge. The rest," as Hillel said, "is commentary; go and study." In Chapter Five we directly address the element of support. An inner contradiction—visible to us as a contradiction—is potentially a valuable source of challenge.

We concluded the last chapter by reminding ourselves that a rich curriculum is filled with the kind of problems we not only cannot but ought not solve too quickly. Why? Because the problems from which we stand to learn are the ones we don't so much solve as let solve us. They cause us, in some way, to change our minds. These are the "good problems" we all need. We wondered in that chapter what can help us create, out of our own problematic behavior (identified in column two), the stuff of good problems from which we can learn. In this chapter we answer that question: the first three languages, taken together, create the stuff of a good problem.

From the Language of New Year's
Resolutions to the Language of Competing Commitments.

Language of New Year's Resolutions	Language of Competing Commitments
• Expresses sincere and genuine intentions	• Expresses genuinely held countervailing commitments
• Creates wishes and hopes for the future	• Creates an inner contradiction or map of an immune system
• But contains little power	• Contains enormous (locked up) power
• Intent is to eliminate or reduce the hindering, problematic behavior	• Intent is to identify the source of that behavior
• The problematic behavior is frequently regarded as a sign of weakness, or shameful ineffectiveness	• Identifies a commitment to self-protection on behalf of which the problematic behavior is *effective,* consistent, faithful, even brilliant
• Assumes that eliminating the problematic behavior will lead to the accomplishment of (first column) commitments or goals	• Recognizes that merely trying to alter problematic behavior is unlikely to accomplish goals
• Frequently attributes less effective change to other people, unanticipated obstacles, or insufficient self-control	• Recognizes the complex, contradictory nature of one's own intentions
• Nontransformational, rarely leads to significant change despite sincere intentions	• Transformational; paradoxically increases the possibility of significant change by making clear the immune system that makes change so difficult

If you have been playing along at home and have now filled in the first three columns for yourself, you can begin to see a first-draft map of an immune system in which you have been living. Instead of being wholly within it, and therefore like a fish in water, this new technology you have built has begun to operate enough to give you the beginning of a picture of the system itself. Paradoxically, the capacity to see the system first of all gives you better understanding of why (if everything stays as it is) real change is unlikely and, secondly, creates the initial step toward real change (because everything is no longer as it was). Just being able to see the system makes us less captive of it. But of course, to bring about real change—a negentropic leap of imagination—we must disturb the balance, not merely look at it. To increase our chances of disturbing the balance, we must ask more of our new technology. It must offer some tool or device by which we can potentially disturb the very foundation of our status quo: preserving equilibrium. To do this, we need a fourth language.

Chapter Four

From the Language of Big Assumptions That Hold Us to the Language of Assumptions We Hold

Disturbing the Immunity to Change

Our four-column technology for personal learning may not be complete yet, but it has begun to take on a discernible shape: it names an inner contradiction we live in and compose. It provides a map of our own captivating equilibrium. It portrays our immune system preventing change. We could also call it a kind of "mental machine" we have carefully built but not yet had a chance to plug in. What happens if you run this mental machine? The answer: it probably produces what we call a Big Assumption.

The Default Mode: Assumptions Taken as Truths

What is a Big Assumption? In our language, an assumption is "big" if we do not actually take it as an assumption but instead as the truth. The dictionary tells us an assumption is something whose truth status is uncertain; it may or may not be true. But Big Assumptions are the ones we take as true. We believe—that is, we take it as unquestioningly so—that water is wet, that tables are hard, and, for example, that if we confront someone and he becomes terribly angry or terribly upset . . . well, it will simply be the end of the world. We do not hold our beliefs about conflict, let's say (or how people feel about us, or whether we remain in control, or whatever appears in our third column), as mere assumptions. We hold them as the truth. Assumptions-taken-as-truth are what we mean by Big Assumptions. They are not so much the assumptions we have as they are the assumptions *that have us.*

Our Big Assumptions come close to naming an ineffable, hard-to-grasp thing: something like the meaning-regulative principles by which we shape the world in which we live. The close work that we (the authors) have done with people around these language forms leads us to a deeply sympathetic conviction: most people are carrying on about as bravely and effectively as they can within the world of their assumptive designs. You have probably met or worked with people whom you see operating dysfunctionally, destructively, or self-destructively. We are suggesting that if you could accurately discern the Big Assumptions under which these people are operating, you might not feel their behavior was any less destructive or self-destructive, but you would feel that at least you understood their behavior. We might even say, "If I held those same Big Assumptions, I might very well be acting in just these destructive ways myself."

Big Assumptions in Childhood . . .

The notion that people form their own constructions of reality underlies much of the delight we take in the stories we tell about children. Two little kids are coming home from school one day, after learning about the Hindu culture. One of them is quite taken with the logo of the universe in which the world is seated upon the back of an elephant and the elephant upon the back of a turtle. "I can understand how the world is on an elephant," the child says, "and how the elephant is on a turtle. But then what does the turtle stand on?" The other child is apparently less perplexed by all this. "I think," she says, "that from then on, it's turtles all the way down."

Or: a soon-to-be-six-year-old is asked by his parents what he wants for his birthday, and they are shocked to hear him say he'd like Tampax. Being good modern parents, however, they decide to engage him in conversation. "Well, why would you want Tampax for your birthday?" they ask. "Because with Tampax," comes the reply, "you can go horseback riding, you can go water skiing, you can do anything!"

Underneath our amusement at these stories there is perhaps a slightly condescending premise. Children's minds, we imply, are charming or cute in part because they only dimly or incompletely grasp how the real world works. A big difference between children and us adults, we further imply, is that they don't quite get it yet, but *we do*. They see through a glass darkly, and we see things as they really are. This is the same kind of thinking that makes the concept of the grown-up appear to be a sensible one—that there are two kinds of people in the world, those who are still growing and developing (and in need of our sympathetic and talented supports) and those who are all grown up. Done. (Dead, practically, but no one tells us that, so we still get up in the morning, put on our clothes, and head off to work.)

. . . and Big Assumptions in Adulthood

In contrast, we (the authors) regard the concept of the grown-up as not very helpful or accurate. We don't believe children alone are the sole purveyors of worldviews that come to be outgrown. We don't believe children are the only ones about whom such stories can be told. In the 1750s the British passed a calendar reform stating that on September 1 of that year the date would become September 12. Thousands of people protested passionately to their government that they were being robbed of twelve days of their lives! (We mentioned this recently to a friend of ours who chuckled briefly and then confessed, under her breath, "Still, I wouldn't like that either, since September is my favorite time of year in New England, with the fall foliage and all, and I'd hate to see the season shortened.")

More recently, the British passed a monetary reform, changing from the old pence to the new pence system. A study was done of how the elderly were adjusting to the change, and one such gentleman observed, "I think it's much too hard for us old people. Why couldn't they just have waited until all the old people died?"

An Australian woman doing a year's sabbatical in this country told us how much difficulty she had adjusting to driving in the United States. "It's not just that you drive on the wrong side of the road," she said. "Even your steering wheels are on the wrong side. I can't tell you how many times I'd pile in to the front *right* side of the car, only to rediscover I needed to get out, and walk around to the other door. One time my mind was on six other things; I got into the front right side, took out my keys, and looked up. 'My God,' I said to myself, 'here in the United States things have gotten so bad, they are even stealing steering wheels!'"

Of course, the countervailing evidence was just an arm's length to her left, but—and here is the main point—*why should one look?* If we are certain we know how the world works—and this is how a Big Assumption operates: it creates certainty—why would we even think to look for a different reality?

The circumstance of becoming so attached to our perspectives that we take them as reality itself is not, in our view, the province of children alone. Stepping out of our perspective may be every bit as difficult, perhaps even more so, for adults as for children. One morning a mother was getting breakfast for her son on a school day. She heard no signs of readiness coming from his bedroom. She went to see how he was doing and found his door closed shut.

"Are you OK?" she asked.

"I'm fine," she heard him say in a very defiant voice. "I'm just not going to school today."

"Well, then," said his mother, "how about you give me three good reasons why you don't want to go to school?"

"I don't like school," she heard him say. "The teachers don't like me. And I'm afraid of the kids. That's three."

"That is three," the mother agreed. "Now I'm going to give you three good reasons why you *are* going to go to school. First, I'm your mother, and I say school is important. Second, you're fifty-three years old. And third, you're principal of the school!"

So it can be difficult to "leave home" at any age. We refer, of course, to the homes, or the bedrooms, of our established habits of minds, which we furnish and make familiar, and leave only warily.

A Mini-Exercise to Illustrate the Default Mode

Here's a quick, stylized experience of how difficult it can be to separate ourselves from our perspectives. (This was shown to us by Linda Booth-Sweeney.) Point your pen (or your finger) up toward the ceiling and trace a circle in a clockwise direction, as if you were drawing it on the ceiling. Keep tracing the circle in a clockwise direction. Now (while continuing to keep the pen moving in the same clockwise direction) slowly move the vertical column of your arm straight down—with the pencil or finger always pointing straight up—until the circle is being traced at chest level. Keep the circle going. Now look down on the circle from above it. Which way is the pen going now? *Counter*clockwise, right?

When we do this in large groups, invariably, amidst the laughter, someone answers, "It's going the other way!"

"It's" going the other way? All right, go ahead and try it again. This time be careful as you move your arm down and lower the pen from pointing over your head to pointing under your chin. Don't switch the direction in which you rotate the pen. Keep it going in a clockwise direction. What happens when you look down on the circle this time? "It" has still "switched" to counterclockwise, hasn't it?

It's so difficult to separate ourselves from our perspective that even if our perspective does change (as this little exercise trickily gets us to do) we may be inclined to feel that it is *the world* rather than *our way of looking at the world* that has changed ("*It's* going the other way!").

Much of what goes under the banner of professional development amounts to helping us develop more skills or capacities to cope, but cope within the worlds of our assumptive designs. The design itself is never in question, or even visible. Transformational approaches to professional development such as ours help us take up a position ever more frequently *outside* the world of our assumptive design, so that we can actually hold on to, and look at, the very principle by which the design itself is being shaped.

Of course, this is not an easy thing to do. As we make our way further into this book, we address quite practical means by which we can strengthen the mental muscle that permits us to look at these assumptions that most often form the lenses through which we see. But why should it be so difficult a thing to do? Looking at our assumptions amounts to uncoupling "reality" from "our way of shaping reality." It amounts to considering that our "perspectives" are not necessarily the same as "the thing itself."

This is the classic philosophical distinction between phenomena (shaped reality, our experience of a thing) and noumena (the essence of the thing itself). It is the distinction underlying the contemporary idea of *constructivism,* that human beings are actively making sense, shaping reality, organizing experience. "Organisms *organize,*" psychologist William Perry said, "and what human organisms organize is meaning." The philosopher and novelist Aldous Huxley wrote that "our experience is not what happens to us, but what we *make* of what happens to us."

The Fourth Language: From the Truths That Hold Us to the Assumptions We Hold

The first step toward sustaining a relationship to our perspectives (rather than being captive of our perspectives) is by surfacing our Big Assumptions. The mental machines we have each constructed can help us do just that. How so? Take another look at what you have written in your third column (by going back to your written work from the first three chapters). The material is here to compose an assumptive sentence stem, the first part of a declaration of your own Big Assumption. If there is a negative in your third-column commitment (for instance, "I'm committed to *not* being seen as holier-than-thou"), then remove the negative by modifying the words, to form a sentence stem like this: "I assume that if I were to be seen as holier-than-thou, then. . . ."

If there is no negative in your third-column commitment (say, "I'm committed to avoiding all conflict at all costs"), then add negative wording, to form a sentence stem like this: "I assume that if I did not avoid all conflict, then. . . ."

After we build the sentence stem, the next job is to complete the sentence quickly and honestly: *How would I feel, then?*

Consult your third column and, using these guidelines, enter an assumptive stem (up to the word "then . . .") in your fourth column by adding or removing the negative. The caption of the fourth column is "Big Assumption." We invite you now to see if you can make one of your own Big Assumptions emerge by honestly and quickly completing a sentence from the stem in the fourth column. Complete the sentence with whatever comes to mind, writing it in your fourth column.

The fourth column is a gateway to the language of our Big Assumptions. We can begin to see where such a language form may take us by hearing how a number of people complete their sentence stems.

As the first step, let's see how the three people we've been following throughout (their first three columns are in Figure 3.5 at the end of Chapter Three) derived the sentence stem from their third-column sentences.

For the first person, the negative language "Not being seen as the Brave Crusader . . ." became "I assume that if people did see me as. . . ."

The second person's negative "Not having our work product be less than I think I could do on my own . . ." became the stem "I assume that if the quality of our work, when I transfer authority, does fall below what I could produce. . . ."

The third person converted the positive language "Avoiding all conflict, at all costs" into a negative stem: "I assume if I did not avoid conflict, then. . . ."

So here's what all three people wrote in their fourth columns (given here in the same order):

> I assume that if people did see me as a Righteous Crusader, Castrating Bitch, or Holier-Than-Thou, then I would eventually be completely shunned, have no real connections in my office other than the most formal and functional, and actually I'd find work a nightmare from which I couldn't wake up.

> I assume that if the quality of our work, when I transfer authority, does fall below what I could produce by maintaining more control, then I will be seen as a failure.

> I assume if I did not avoid conflict, then I will find myself becoming uncontrollably angry.

Of course, these are the Big Assumptions for three individuals. Your fourth-column Big Assumption is unique to you. We have found it interesting that even when people have similar assumptive stems, completion of the stems can yield quite different sentences. For example, several people might begin with a stem like the third one but go on to quite different completions:

I assume if I did not avoid conflict, then . . .

. . . I would regularly experience myself as outmaneuvered and ineffectual.

. . . I would be constantly anxious and preoccupied.

. . . others would be quickly drawn in with their own conflicts, and all friendly feelings would vanish at work.

. . . I would learn things about how others feel that would be devastating, and I would never get over it.

. . . I'd be in tears.

A Checkpoint in Using the Fourth Language

As different as these last five Big Assumptions are, they have something in common. Different as the three that preceded this last sampling are, they too have something in common. Different as your own Big Assumption may be from any of these, it most likely shares a common feature with them as well. That is: when you come to the end of the sentence, the stated consequences are usually quite dire. Big Assumptions generally take the form:

> I assume that if this thing were to happen that I have long been working hard to keep from happening, then . . . er, well, . . . I would just *die*! (or: . . . someone else would just *die*! or: . . . it would be the end of the world!)

In other words, these Big Assumptions take us into highly consequential, decidedly nontrivial territory. Our sense of dire consequence or fundamental violation may even be quickly followed by the thought, "But I know that actually this is probably not so." Yet we have to admit we are operating as if it *were* so. Whatever rational disclaimers we might bring to our own Big Assumption, we also have to acknowledge that, in some powerful nether region, it holds sway over us.

Or perhaps our response to our Big Assumption, once we see it before our eyes, is, "And this is *not* just 'an assumption'; this is for sure the truth!" It may well be. But it may also *not* be. The certainty we experience hints at the phenomenology of what it means for our Big Assumptions to "have us" rather than our having them.

One thing for sure: we will never have an opportunity to explore whether the Big Assumption is true or not until we put it before ourselves where we can look at it, and begin to create a relationship to it.

The Big Assumptions bring us, like Indiana Jones, before our own Temple of Doom. They seem to warn us about the ways in which our universe could be disturbed. They suggest how our more primitive gods (not necessarily those we worship politely at church, synagogue, or mosque) might be cosmically offended, causing them to hurl lightning bolts at us.

The language of our Big Assumptions explicitly declared is a wonderfully refreshing, seldom-heard, but instantaneously recognizable form of speech. When we invite people in large groups to let us in on the content of their fourth columns (if they wish), the things we hear cause us to laugh; or they cause us to ooh and ahh in the light of their piercing clarity, or the courage of their honesty, or the valuable company of their familiarity; or they cause us to be silent in contemplation of the proliferating implications even one previously invisible Big Assumption can set off:

> I assume if I learn more about what people are *really* doing who work for me, then I will be responsible to act upon a million more things and I will drown under the weight of it all.

> I assume if people feel completely comfortable with me, and I become a more and more accepted and integrated member of this group, then I will become what I hate, one of Them, and lose my identification with, and connection to, my own people.

> I assume if I tell people what I really think, then I'll be fired, unhirable, broke, and my family will sleep in the streets.

> I assume that if I really did make time to act on my goal, then I'd discover I'm not able to accomplish it.

> I assume that if I were really to take a look at aspects of myself I'm hiding from my awareness, then I would so loathe myself as to not be able to go on.

> I assume that if I were to really deal with it, then I'd have to decide to quit my job. (Or: my marriage)

I assume that if I refuse to participate in the gossip, then I will no longer have people coming to me, and I will lose the way I have come to feel valued and special at work.

The Four-Column Conceptual Map
as a More Adequate "Problem Space"

You have now completed a first-draft version of the four-column conceptual map of your mental machine, your new technology for personal learning. Our work together is far from over; in fact, it is just beginning. But how should we understand what we have made so far?

The conceptual map is certainly not a solution to the problem that is created in the first column, namely, that we genuinely hold commitments we have not yet realized. Rather, the map (and the language forms to which it points us) creates a more complete, more satisfying space in which to consider and experience this problem. In a sense, far from having been solved, the problem has grown! We have widened it out, and explored its roots. Rather than focusing like a laser on the solution to a specific problem, we have dug up ground all around the problem and made a big mess. But we have done so on behalf of specific functional (and educational, psychological, and leadership) ideas.

The functional idea is that highly localized and apparently inexpensive solutions to some problems are often highly ineffective and uneconomical because the problems recur in differing forms.

The educational idea is that some problems, if we can bear to stay in relation to them and not solve them too quickly, can teach us a great deal. We can use them to solve us.

The psychological idea is that the underlying architecture or transformational grammar of qualitative change (genuinely negentropic development) is the movement from subject to object—that is, the movement of our meaning making from a place where we are its captive to a place where we can look at it, reexamine it, and possibly alter it.

The leadership idea is that we are not able to effect any significant change until we recognize the dynamic immune system by which *we* continuously manufacture *nonchange*.

Each four-column conceptual map, read backwards, has a powerful story to tell (Figure 4.1). Holding as true the Big Assumption
of our fourth columns, we are understandably committed to pro-
tecting ourselves in ways indicated by our third columns. Faithfully,
effectively, even brilliantly living out these third-column commitments, we act in the fashion reflected in our second column, which
consistently and constantly undermines our capacity to fully realize other kinds of genuinely held commitments (such as those appearing in our first columns). This may be the road to hell, but in
drawing a fuller map we may discover a way to get off.

It is a fuller map because the usual approach to reflection does
not get beyond the second column. We articulate a goal, a vision,
or commitment (column one) and discover by some means how
we are keeping the goal, vision, or commitment from being realized (column two), but then what? We conscientiously move to
eliminate the offending behaviors of column two. We seek to
shrink them as if they were a cancer or tumor.

Lessons for Leaders:
The Dynamic Equilibrium at the Organizational Level

We can see this at a collective level if we look at any effort to effect organizational change. Let's consider one of the most common (and admirable) organizational aspirations of present-day
life in America: the commitment to greater respect for diversity
or inclusivity. Once sufficient consensus gathers for this aspiration, the organization has a viable mission: a shared column-one
commitment. Classrooms and offices, schools and workplaces
take up the commitment that people of diverse races, genders,
ethnicities, sexual orientations, learning abilities, and physical capacities should feel comfortably and respectfully included. "No
subgroup should feel silenced or excluded" is another way the
commitment is expressed, an aspiration that reflects the best of
the democratic American experiment. In fulfillment of the commitment, effective leaders may help their organizations engage—
often bravely and painfully—in forms of institutional self-reflection
(sometimes called diversity audits). These bring to light instances
of how the organization, or its policies, practices, or members,

Figure 4.1. Four-Column Versions of the Map.

1 Commitment	2 What I'm Doing or Not Doing That Prevents My Commitment from Being Fully Realized	3 Competing Commitment	4 Big Assumption
I am committed to the value or the importance of . . .		I may also be committed to . . .	I assume that if . . .
More open and direct communication at work.	*I don't speak up when people are violating the norm I value. Silently, I collude in it being OK to talk behind one another's back.*	*Not being seen as the Brave Crusader, Castrating Bitch, or Miss Holier-Than-Thou; . . . having people feel comfortable with me.*	*People did see me as a Righteous Crusader, Castrating Bitch, or Holier-Than-Thou, then I would eventually be completely shunned, have no real connections in my office other than the most formal and functional, and actually I'd find work a nightmare from which I couldn't wake up.*
Supporting my staff to exercise more individual initiative.	*(1) When they ask me to get involved or take over, I don't refuse. (2) I don't delegate as much as I could. (3) I too often am willing to be drawn into things when I should refer to the subordinate who is in charge of that area.*	*Not having my staff feel like I've abandoned them; not having my staff unhappy with me; not having our work product be less than I think I could do on my own, even if it means disempowering or failing to empower my staff.*	*The quality of our work, when I transfer authority, does fall below what I could produce by maintaining more control, then I will be seen as a failure.*
Securing sufficient resources and additional personnel support to thrive (rather than barely survive) in my job.	*I don't or can't say NO!*	*Avoiding all conflict, at all costs.*	*I did not avoid conflict, then I will find myself becoming uncontrollably angry.*

intentionally or unintentionally exclude or silence members of its own community. The activities constitute an exercise of the second language, an institutional version of the language of responsibility, and the lists of offending instances constitute second-column entries in our map. Now what?

The perfectly logical, understandable, and even courageous next step is to set about seeking to reduce this "list of shame," these barriers to change; to strike, one by one, the offending organizational or individual violations of the commitment. The effective, conscientious leader or leadership team, having diagnosed a cancerous tumor on the body of the institution, sets about to apply the organizational equivalent of chemotherapy or radiation to shrink this tumor to as small a size as possible. As we say, this is logical, understandable, commendably conscientious and brave. Experience, however, shows that it has one small flaw: it doesn't work. We have, in effect, taken a New Year's Resolution approach to the barriers in our way.

Our own suggestion of a more effective next step—exercising the third language—is admittedly less linear and more counterintuitive. What if leaders next tried to build a "container" that is safe enough to *hold on* to these hard-won second-column recognitions? What if they do this so that the system, or its members, can learn about the other competing commitments, internal contradictions, and Big Assumptions to which they direct us, which are living in our midst, and which are giving rise to these behaviors? Without an unashamed (dare we say inclusive?) stance toward these behaviors—so that they can lead us to their bigger sources— "organizational cleansing" on behalf of diversity becomes a kind of politically correct weed killer that knocks out, though only temporarily, the surface manifestations. New strains, often stronger and more resistant, soon appear.

It takes an extraordinary leader to cultivate a language for surfacing organizational contradictions in a fashion that does not end up scapegoating some segment of the whole. It may not even be possible for organizations to take up this exploration of their systemwide contradictions and Big Assumptions without a number of their members exploring the same at an individual level. This brings us to the possibility that in constructing the four-column conceptual map—in drawing this fuller account of our own road to hell—we may also have found a clue to getting off the road.

"Looking At" Versus
"Looking Through" the Big Assumption

The work you have done so far has enabled you to make contact with one of your own inner contradictions and one of your own Big Assumptions. If you ask us what we think the effect might be on your own meaning making and future behavior, our answer is that we expect there will be *no* effect, none whatsoever, *unless* you take some kind of action to protect and preserve your relationship to these potentially transformative issues.

In the absence of such supports, our prediction is that you will tend to come away from this process thinking something like, "Hmmm. That was provocative and interesting. I need to think more about that. I should think more about that. I *will* think more about that . . . tomorrow." Like Scarlett O'Hara in *Gone with the Wind,* we will think about it "tomorrow."

"Give me strength, O Lord," said St. Augustine, "to live a purer life—but not just yet!" The issues you have identified here will recede from view. They will move into what Buddhism calls "the sea of forgetfulness." They will be gone with the wind. What you have temporarily made visible—through your hard work with this new technology—what you have made the object of your attention, you will become reidentified with, until it becomes again the way you see; not something you look at but something you see through, your lens on the world.

So, what do we need most to stay in relationship to these ideas? We need colleagues, first of all, simply to help us remember, to keep present at the door the troubling ideas that tempt us out of the bedrooms of our established habits of mind, so we can be in relation to them. We have often found in the ongoing learning groups we facilitate (sometimes people call them "assumption groups" or "transformational learning groups") that when people reconvene, sometimes several weeks after first elaborating their four-column maps, they are embarrassed to confess that they cannot even recall their inner contradictions.

Why is this? We do not believe it is merely because these people are so busy they lack the space to remember one more thing. We think it is a perfect example of what psychologists call repression. Repression is *purposeful* forgetting, forgetting for a very good reason, usually for the reason that remembering is going to cause us trouble. In this case it's the trouble of having to leave the bedrooms of an established habit of mind (as the Calvin and Hobbes cartoon suggests).

We need colleagues, willing partners, people we can talk to, whom we listen to and who listen to us. We need a little "new language community," where forms of speech viscous enough to suspend this kind of experience can be practiced and protected, keeping in mind that a community can be as small as two people.

So what might go on in these intentional language communities, aside from making use of each other to remember the inner contradictions and Big Assumptions that can so easily slip from view? Later, in Chapter Eight, we bring you directly into the life of such groups and the kind of continued learning an active relationship to these languages can promote. But for now, perhaps it is useful simply to get a quick picture of the kind of work they entail, so that you can see what it might mean to use our maps to get off the road of good intentions and discover a different destination than the place to which the road so often leads. There are four basic steps in the process of working to *look at* rather than *through* our Big Assumptions.

Step One: Observing Ourselves in Relation to the Big Assumption

After people have elaborated their four-column maps and have begun to let each other in on their inner contradictions and Big Assumptions, we suggest they complete an assignment before the group next meets (this could be after a week, two weeks, or even a month): we ask people not to try to make any changes in their thinking or their behavior, but just to become better observers of themselves in relation to their Big Assumptions. Specifically, we ask them to notice and keep track of what does or does not occur as a consequence of holding their Big Assumptions as true. The group reconvenes and people have an opportunity to tell and listen to stories about what was noticed.

These accounts, like most group meetings, have much the same quality as the conversations that ensue in creating the four-column conceptual map; there is usually a lot of laughter and appreciation for the truthful and familiar depictions of who we really

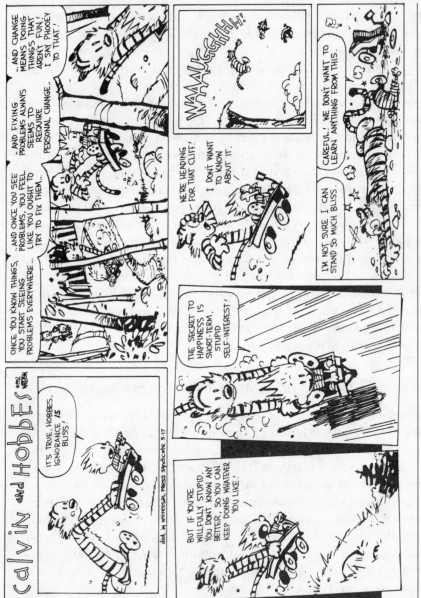

are in our fully complicated glory, a way we too seldom have the opportunity to present ourselves.

The theme that tends to run through this particular meeting is how much of our living and choosing and experiencing is influenced by our holding our Big Assumptions as true. We see our Big Assumption showing up in areas we expected to see it, but also in places where it was quite unexpected. This usually creates added energy to continue the exploration. We tend to be more curious about something that we notice having such a big influence on our living. Curiosity is the high-test fuel for the engine of learning.

Step Two: Actively Looking for Experiences That Cast Doubt on Our Big Assumptions

When people are ready, we assign another kind of homework. We ask them, again in the interval between meetings, not to try changing any of their thinking or behavior, but this time to be on the lookout for any experiences that cast some doubt on the truthfulness of their assumptions. Assumptions-taken-as-true have the quality of universal generalizations, which we all know are supposed to be disprovable by even a single counterinstance.

In psychological reality, we run up against counterinstances to our Big Assumptions all the time. But without a language space that preserves and protects them, they are quite unlikely to pose any problem at all for our universal generalizations. Why is that? Because we are a tricky lot, and we systematically disattend to these otherwise troubling pieces of evidence casting shadows over our precious premises.

Our Big Assumptions are like favorite hypotheses, and we are like the sort of scientists who, should they meet disconfirming data, say in effect, "Well, so much the worse for the data!" Out it goes, and the precious hypothesis is preserved. If we, on the other hand, vigilantly seek to collect such counterinstances, bring these specimens back to our group for inspection, and have the opportunity to talk and think and laugh about them, we take one more step toward building a relationship to the assumption rather than being run by it.

Step Three: Exploring the History of Our Big Assumptions

The third curricular move in our groups is for people to spend some time between meetings reflecting on the "biography" of their Big Assumption. When was it born? How long have you lived with this assumption? Where do you think it got its start? What early, and possibly not recently examined, foundation does it rest on? How satisfactory a foundation does this seem to you to be in the present day?

The conversations that follow our work on this third assignment usually take us back into people's earlier life experience. We find that the Big Assumptions often got their start long ago, long before people's current jobs, usually long before they became grown-ups. They usually get their start in families of origin, when we are little people, with little power, and the world in which we are seeking to thrive is a world largely defined by our families.

These conversations do not necessarily lead to dissatisfaction with our Big Assumptions, but they do usually lead to dissatisfaction with the foundations on which they rest. We recognize that although the Big Assumption may have been true in the earlier world, and may still be true in our current world, the foundation upon which it rests is no longer appropriate to the present day, now that we have considerably greater power than we did as children and now that the world in which we live is considerably less shaped and defined by our parents and families of origin. We may still reconfirm the long-held Big Assumption, but we need a new foundation for it, one more fitting to the realities of the present day and our present selves.

Step Four: Designing and Running a Safe, Modest Test of the Assumption

The fourth curricular move involves inviting group members to design a modest and safe test of their Big Assumptions. Should they decide to run these tests, this involves the first real action in the world, an altering of one's usual conduct, for purposes of seeing what happens, that is, gaining information that can be reflected upon, individually and within the group, in light of the Big Assumption. Here we consider taking actions we would not normally permit ourselves in holding our Big Assumptions as true.

It is important that the proposed experiment be a safe one. We use the group as a collective mind to consider what might happen, and whether—if our worst suspicions are confirmed—the costs of this information are not too great. We do not want to be running tests for which the cost of the findings risks our continued effectiveness or the well-being of our organizations. We are not suggesting people bring themselves to what they believe is the edge of a flat world, clasp their hands in the small of their backs, bend their knees and leap off to what they think may be their deaths.

This is why we refer to these experiments as modest and safe. They usually begin with quite tiny, novel moves to see what we learn. This often involves seeking feedback from a single, trusted colleague (for example, trying out new behaviors in a staff meeting and asking a friend to give you her impressions of how others respond).

These tests involve keeping our weight firmly balanced on what we are sure is solid ground, and carefully sticking a toe over the edge of the world we have created by our assumptive designs to see whether indeed there is nothing but space beyond the edge, or whether, as Columbus's crew discovered, the world may be shaped differently than we had imagined. These tests, once reviewed and perhaps refined in the groups, may then be run, and successive group meetings consider the findings and their meanings for our Big Assumptions. A round of modest tests might be followed by tests of a slightly bigger kind. As we come to trust there is firm ground beyond the imagined limits of our Big Assumptions, we shift our weight and move out onto new spaces. By such small steps, we emerge from the bedrooms of our established habits of mind.

Building Up Space Between the (No Longer) Big Assumption and Ourselves

These curricular moves have similar intentions. They are all about gradually building up a psychological space between ourselves and our Big Assumptions in order to move them from subject to object, where we can look at them, turn them around in our hands, and consider altering them. The usual result of such work is not that people slap their foreheads and declare their Big Assumptions entirely false. What more often happens is the sort of thing that is common to adulthood. We add qualifications to our assumptions— riders, amendments, attachments, exceptions. We say, "I still hold my Big Assumption as basically true—but under certain circumstances, with these people, under these conditions, I can suspend my Big Assumption temporarily."

Such small changes might lead to bigger changes, but what has been most impressive to us is the way that even quite small changes in our Big Assumptions can lead to quite large changes in our sense of our possibilities, the choices and moves we can consider making. Even small changes in our Big Assumptions can have big implications for permanently altering our once-captivating equilibrium.

From the Language of Big Assumptions That Hold Us to the Language of Assumptions That We Hold.

Language of Big Assumptions That Hold Us	Language of Assumptions That We Hold
• Automatically produced, without intention or awareness (the meanings to which we are subject)	• Produced only with difficulty, creating space or distance between self and one's meanings (the meanings we can relate to as object)
• Assumptions inhabited as truths	• Assumptions taken as assumptions
• Creates a sense of certainty, that one's perspective *is* reality	• Creates valuable doubt, the opportunity to question, explore, test, reconfirm or revise one's assumption
• Anchors and sustains our immune system	• Creates a pivotal lever for disturbing our immunity to change
• Names the terms by which we would understand our universe to be catastrophically disturbed or violated (our "Temple of Doom")	• Makes the catastrophic consequences a proposition available for testing
• Nontransformational; maintains the world as we have been constructing it	• Transformational; changes the world as we understand it to be, and our sense of our possibilities within it

Hopefully, even this quick sketch of a new kind of learning group makes clear that its purpose is quite different from that of providing a kind of collegial support that surfaces difficulties and uses the resources of group members' collective experience to propose solutions to them. Such groups can no doubt extend a kind of help ("I once had a difficulty like that. This is what I tried, which worked well for me. . . ."). When people identify the limitations of such groups, what they usually say is that advice giving has the inevitable constraint that the giver is a different person from the problem poser, and that the situation from which the giver speaks is often importantly different from that of the problem poser.

But a bigger constraint is that such groups, even if the advice is good, go on entirely within each person's assumptive "box." The groups are more about solving problems than learning from them. They are not about finding a way to sift through them to locate good problems, the sort that can solve us. To do this, we need a kind of technology that makes the assumptions themselves the object of our attention and exploration.

Ongoing participation in a language community of this sort leads to building up relationships to not just one Big Assumption but several. With help, we can build a nest of Big Assumptions. The nest metaphor is chosen deliberately. At times, this may feel like a hornet's nest. We may feel stung by what our new reflecting stirs up. But the image of a nest of assumptions also evokes a home for hatching new life, new forms, new ways of making meaning that— if nurtured—one day take wing.

How to Regard the Messy Work of the First Four Languages

Such a home can feel messy, dangerous, unwelcome. There is an old Russian story that comes to mind to help us remember how to regard such messy nests. One day a woodsman set out to the forest to chop wood. As he walked across the icy expanse, he spied a little bird freezing to death on the frozen tundra. He took pity on it, picked it up, and held it close as he made his way to the forest. The little bird drew warmth from his body and began to come back to life.

But when the woodsman reached the forest, he had a problem. He needed both arms free to cut down the trees, and both arms free to carry the wood home. He could no longer keep the bird, but he did not want to reconsign it to the icy end from which he had just saved it. He was unsure what to do next.

Then he noticed in the distance that a herd of cattle must have recently passed by because they had left their brown, round calling cards dotting the horizon. The woodsman thought the solution to his problem might be found in these cowpies, still fresh and steaming in the arctic air.

He walked over and selected the biggest, steamiest cowpie he could find and nestled the bird into it. He went on with his business, chopped his wood, and headed home.

Our friend, the little bird, hunkered down into his new home—this rich, fragrant, fertile, organic environment, such as any of us might feel we ourselves work in from time to time. The little bird drew warmth from this nest and came back to life. He began to feel so good that he threw back his little head and sang his song into the universe. He sung so well and so loud that a wolf, traveling not far away, followed the sound to its source, plucked the little bird out of its home, and ate it for lunch.

That's the whole story, but like all good Russian stories it has not one moral but three. The first moral is that whoever gets you into a great big stinking mess like the one you have is not necessarily your enemy. The second is that whoever gets you out of such a mess is not necessarily your friend. And the third moral: when you're up to your neck in it—*don't sing!*

Part Two

The Social Languages
Maintaining and Upgrading the Machine

Chapter Five

From the Language of Prizes and Praising to the Language of Ongoing Regard

In the first four chapters, by way of the four internal languages, you have built a custom-designed machine, a new technology for personal learning and leadership on behalf of transformational change. Later in this book, we return to this machine to explore its operation further.

Right now, though, as with any good machine, if you come to sense its value you will be interested in *maintaining* it. And if it possesses the potentially regenerative capacities of today's best technologies, you will be interested in knowing how it can be *upgraded*.

The next three chapters introduce you to three more languages, whose purpose is to help maintain and upgrade the technology built in the first part of this book. The first of these social languages addresses the subject of *support* and facilitates a transformation from support as the unexamined entitlement to confer worthiness on another into self-disclosing personal regard.

Nearly every organization or work team we've been privileged to spend time with has been averse to public expression of conflict. This was no surprise to us, and we doubt it comes as any surprise to you. After all, it can be a difficult and uncomfortable thing to directly tell or hear from someone about a rift, upset, or disagreement between the two of you. (In fact, productive and even growth-facilitating expression of conflict is a high art, rarely well practiced, and one we save for the seventh and last language.) But what has surprised us is this: nearly every organization or work team we've

spent time with also astonishingly undercommunicates the genuinely positive, appreciative, and admiring experiences of its members. This is more puzzling. It is also a terrible deprivation of the
vitality of a work setting. As we said in Chapter Four, a setting rich
for transformational learning must include a special blend of challenge and support.

The Value of Being Valued

We all do better at work if we regularly have the experience that
what we do matters, that it is valuable, and that our presence makes
a difference to others. We may know in our hearts that what we do
matters, but it is certainly confirming to hear the words from others. We do not, after all, work and live in a vacuum. Believing that
what we do and how we do it makes a difference can also lead us
to take additional care in performing our work.

Perhaps more important, hearing that our work is valued by
others can confirm for us that we matter as a person. It connects
us to other people. This is no small matter in organizations where
the pace and intensity of work can lead a person to feel isolated.
This sense that we signify may be one of our deepest hungers. One
way we experience that what we are doing at work is valuable is by
hearing regularly from others how they value what we do. But what
is the usual quality of such communication?

A Quick Exercise: Step One

Stop reading for thirty seconds and turn your attention to your colleagues at work. See if you can bring to awareness any experience
of valuing a coworker's relatively recent behavior. It doesn't have
to be a huge, life-changing thing. In fact, it could be one of those
tiny, everyday occurrences that seem relatively insignificant but that
make a difference to how the day, or the hour, goes. Take thirty
seconds or however long you need to do this. Don't read on until
you've completed this meditation.

OK. What we'd like you to do is this: imagine yourself in a staff meeting with this person present. Even imagine that your work setting has the norm that people communicate their appreciation to fellow workers and colleagues. Now imagine that one way this is done is through regularly setting aside five minutes or so at the beginning of weekly or biweekly meetings. Imagine that the chair of the meeting has opened the floor for any such expressions anyone might like to deliver.

A Quick Exercise: Step Two

At the top of a sheet of paper, write down exactly what you'd say in this meeting if you were to communicate your admiration or appreciation to your colleague at this time. Don't read on until you've written this down.

Aha: you're reading on without having written anything down, aren't you? (Just a friendly reminder that we really seriously believe you're going to get a lot more out of this book if you take us up on our invitations!)

OK. What you've got there (we hope) is your first effort toward communicating your way of valuing the contribution or effort of another—the language of regard.

We'll return in a moment to what you've written and give you a chance to evaluate it, and perhaps construct it in a way you (and we) would regard as more powerful. But first, let's consider what we the authors have discovered is the usual nature of such communication.

The Default Mode: Indirect, Nonspecific Entitlements to Confer Worthiness upon Another

Although our communication of how another's behaviors, choices, and intentions matter to us at work is rare enough (especially beyond the customary appreciations supervisors hand out to their subordinates), when such communication does occur it commonly sounds like this (spoken to a group):

I'd just like to especially acknowledge Jacqueline's contributions to this effort. She went way beyond the call of duty here and deserves a round of applause from us all.

You were so great in that client meeting yesterday, Angus. I don't know what we would have done without you there.

Thanks, you have been such a great teammate in this project. You are so patient, so flexible, and so smart.

Now, what's wrong with any of this? you might be asking yourself. *I'd be happy just to hear a little more of this kind of communication where I work!* Well, maybe so. If you're feeling this way, it seems to confirm the initial observation as to how undercommunicating most work settings are of the genuine experience of positively valuing another's contributions.

Nonetheless, each of these speeches partakes in one of the three most common ways we drain the power out of such communication. Especially for leaders who would take seriously the opportunity to be language leaders, and to enhance the nature of the languages available at work, it is worth considering how we can foster not merely more language of valuing but a powerful language of valuing.

The Fifth Language: From the Indirect, the Nonspecific, and the Conferring of Attributes to Ongoing Regard

We call the regular expression of genuinely experiencing the value of a coworker's behavior the language of ongoing regard. Ongoing regard has two faces, one of appreciation and the other of admiration. Consider how these two powerful positive feelings have somewhat different qualities and rhythms. When we are expressing appreciation, we let the other person know that we have received something we value. We feel we have been given something—not necessarily a material something—that we are happy to have, or feel benefited by having. When we express admiration, it is less about something of value entering our sphere and more about our taking up temporary residence in the other's sphere. We imaginatively inhabit the other's world and find ourselves instructed, inspired, or in some way enhanced by the other's actions or choices. We have found three qualities that make communication of ongoing regard more powerful.

Being Direct

The first element that seems to make such communication more powerful is directness. Appreciation or admiration is delivered directly to the person, not to others about the person. A common, but dissipating, way of delivering such communication is (like the first of three typical speeches above) to convert the person you are speaking about into a third-person pronoun: "I just want to say a word of appreciation to Marisel. *She* went out of her way to . . ." and so on, the rest of the communication essentially being delivered to everybody but Marisel—while she is cast in the role of a welcome eavesdropper. Although it may be a little more uncomfortable to speak directly to Marisel, especially in front of others, the communication is more powerful for Marisel when delivered this way. Interestingly, for reasons we discuss in a moment, it is also more powerful for everyone else in the room.

Checkpoint: your own directness. Take a minute to look back at what you wrote. Is it direct? Could it be more direct? If yes, how so? Take a minute to rewrite your statement. If you're working with a talk partner, think about what would be most useful to you: to hear his feedback on the directness of your original statement? To hear his reactions to your thoughts about your statement (or to your redesign, if you did one)? To hear his suggestions for how to be more direct? To have him be a good listener? If you are someone's talk partner, and you are asked for your reactions or feedback, try to be as specific as you can.

Being Specific

The second element that makes communicating one's appreciation or admiration more powerful is being specific. As in the second familiar speech above, our communications are often quite general, expressing more about our good feeling than what the other actually did to cause us to feel this way. We might say, "Lee-Beng, about that client meeting we had together last Monday—I thought you were just great. I left feeling so glad you were on this project with us!" The speaker delivered the communication directly to Lee-Beng, who has no idea really what it was he did that made such a difference, or how it made a difference to the speaker. The speaker's comment may lead him to feel good, for the moment, as many of us feel when someone compliments us. The problem is that he can't go any further than this.

Since Lee-Beng is a grown-up, with his own criteria about what is important and valuable, he has no basis to decide whether *he* values or cares about what the speaker is valuing or caring about. Perhaps the speaker is so glad Lee-Beng is a part of the team because he is tall, young, handsome, or well-dressed, or knows how the Red Sox are doing, or comes from the Midwest, and the speaker feels her client garnered a positive impression from one of these attributes or circumstances. If Lee-Beng is working on being valued for his contributions of mind, emotional sensitivity, or leadership ability, he may actually feel little or no benefit from the communication, but it would still be better for him to hear this than to erroneously conclude that he is making a difference in the ways he wishes to.

Alternatively, if Lee-Beng is accustomed to thinking that the speaker tends to value qualities Lee-Beng feels are superficial or out of his control, and then he learns that the speaker was valuing some quality of his mind, emotional sensitivity, or leadership ability, the communication is enormously more valuable and powerful for him if delivered with a specific description of what she was appreciating or admiring.

In both cases, the speaker's specifics give Lee-Beng the opportunity to understand the difference that he makes to that person. Whether he *values* the appreciation as the speaker does is a different consideration, and one that depends on his personal values.

One last benefit of being specific benefits the speaker, who also stands to learn about herself the more specific she is about her appreciation or admiration. This goes back to the point that we are all active meaning makers, and that our values, assumptions, and commitments profoundly influence which pieces we attend to or see, as well as how we put the pieces together—that is, how we make sense of what we see. These meanings in turn dictate how we behave. We can look at our meanings to see what they tell us about our personal values, assumptions, and commitments. This is not the typical level at which we attend to ourselves, but we (the authors) think it is worth the effort because it constitutes an unusually clear window into ourselves. From that window, one can ask critical questions: "Am I doing what I say, think, and believe I'm doing?" "Do I want to do what I see myself doing?" "Why? Why not?"

The speaker who specifically described what she appreciates about Lee-Beng's contributions in the meeting can, for example, begin to ask herself a series of questions that ultimately uncover her personal ideas and ideals about effective leadership. She could start by asking herself what she means by leadership and using the behaviors she deems leaderly in Lee-Beng as a reference point to her meanings. We want to be clear that the point of this is not for her to defend to herself why she thinks what she does about leadership, but rather to use her reactions as a source for learning about herself and her meanings. As in one of the scenarios for Lee-Beng, the speaker could take her thinking a step further by delving into it to ask, "What are some of the key assumptions I am making about leadership and leaderlike behavior? Are they warranted, and how do I know if they are?"

Over time, the speaker could begin to ask herself a more generalized set of questions based on tracking her positive reactions to people: "Which kinds of behaviors do I find myself appreciating and admiring? Is there a pattern to them? For example, are they mostly about people helping my work go more smoothly without attention to the possible costs to them? Do I require that people be good mind readers of my needs and wishes?"

One CEO we worked with discovered, for example, that he directed the majority of his expressions of appreciation toward his managers' *new* initiatives. He was struck by this and began to track his acts of appreciation for further reflection. He then noticed that indeed he was rarely moved by what he intellectually knew was the equally important contribution of maintaining and sustaining worthwhile initiatives already begun. In contrast, he recognized that he was, in fact, most excited by people's ideas for change. He was chagrined to discover the unevenness of his ongoing regard.

In effect, this CEO's reflections on the pattern of his appreciation and admiration led him to make visible to himself yet another intriguing inner contradiction: he was genuinely committed (column one) to the value and importance of acknowledging all kinds of critical contributions his managers made to the success of the company. He began, for the first time, to take responsibility (column two) for the fact that he himself was underacknowledging the critical function of effectively sustaining valuable initiatives begun long ago. He could then identify first a hidden, competing commitment ("I want to feel like we are always doing something new" might go into his third column) and second a juicy Big Assumption that was utterly fascinating to him. The fascination was that he realized how influenced he was by it and how poorly it would stand up to direct scrutiny (column four): "I assume the success of the company depends much more on the *dis*continuous, novel moves we make than on the *continuous*."

This assumption, he saw, anchored an immune system preventing any powerful realization of his first-column commitment. Because he grasped the shortsightedness of his enthusiasms, he began to explore his Big Assumptions and to be more mindful about supporting both "fruit tree shaking" *and* "jelly making." (Interestingly, when he first shared his insight with his managers, they instantly recognized the pattern he described; several people talked about how they felt unappreciated for their successes in keeping their departments running smoothly.)

Checkpoint: your own specificity. It's time now to return to your statement of appreciation. How specific is it? Could it be more specific? If yes, how so? Make any revisions you want, and then check in with your partner if you have one. If you do not, you may want to ask yourself, *What do I learn from making my communication more specific?*

Being Nonattributive

The third and last element that we have found makes communications of appreciation and admiration powerful is that they do not characterize the other's attributes but rather describe the speaker's experience; in shorthand, the communications are nonattributive.

This may be the most difficult of the three to put into practice regularly, in good part because most of us tend to move very quickly from thinking or feeling about what another person does or says—in short, reacting—to making generalizations or characterizations about that person. Ellen says something I find funny, and I think to myself, *That is so funny,* and then, without my necessarily realizing it, I say to myself *Ellen is so funny.* Notice how my initial experience (that I was amused) turns into something about her (now she is funny).

It may seem odd to you that we're urging you not to make statements of this sort: "Carlos, I just want you to know how much I appreciate how generous you are" (or: "what a good sense of humor you have" or "that you always know the right thing to say"), or "Alice, you are so patient" (or, "so prompt," "so never-say-die," "always there when you are needed,"), and so on, like the third speaker at the beginning of this chapter. These seem like such nice things to say to someone. What could possibly be the problem with saying them?

The problem we see is this: the person, inevitably and quite properly, relates what you say to how she knows herself to be. You can tell Carlos he is generous, but he knows how generous he actually is. You can tell Alice she is very patient, but she knows her side of how patient she is being with you.

If we characterize people, even if we do so quite positively, we actually engage—however unintentionally—in the rather presumptuous activity of entitling ourselves to say who and how the other is. We entitle ourselves to confer upon people the sources of their worthiness. We say, "This is the shape of the person," or if we are direct, "This is your shape." We dress the person in a suit of psychological clothes. As much as they might appreciate the fancy quality of the cloth, they are likely to feel, "Well, it doesn't exactly fit. You'd need to let it out a bit here, take it in a lot there." Ultimately, if we appreciate or admire by making attributions or characterizations of the person, we are doing something *to* her; we have pulled on her in one direction or another.

Alternatively, if we limit such communications to express our own experience, we leave the other completely free, not pulled upon, not shaped up, not defined at all. Alan does not learn who Alan is; he learns what your experience of him or his actions is. Instead of "Alan, I appreciate what a generous person you are," we might say, "Alan, I appreciate the way you took all that time to fill me in on what I missed. It made a real difference to me." What happens here? The speaker doesn't characterize Alan at all. The speaker is only talking about her or his experience of Alan. Attributive communication ("You are so generous") is often responded to by correcting the record ("No, I'm not"). But Alan does not have to correct the record because what the speaker says cannot be "wrong" since it is only about the speaker's experience. (No one ever responds to "I learned a lot from watching you in that meeting" with "No, you didn't!")

Many of us long ago learned (or at least heard) the widely promulgated suggestion that we communicate our *negative* experience with *I* statements rather than *you* statements. Communications experts urge us not to say to our spouse, "You are such a slob, the way you just throw your clothes on the floor." Instead, they commend to us the virtues of: "I really feel disrespected by the way you just throw your clothes on the floor as if I'm a maid or something." Why? *You* statements provoke defensiveness; *I* statements characterize the speaker's experience and not the listener. *You* statements require any listener with even a shred of self-respect to repair himself before he can continue in the conversation. ("You haven't even noticed that I've gotten better with that . . .") *I* statements leave the listener unpulled upon, either in the description of his character or in a demand for behavioral change ("This is how I feel; I leave it to you to make a free choice").

The wisdom in the well-known advice to eschew *you* statements in favor of *I* statements when communicating our negative experience also applies when communicating our positive experience. Characterizing the other, even positively, though not necessarily provoking defensiveness does provoke a reaction: having been acted upon, we react. But characterizing our own experience, positive or negative, leaves the other informed (not formed) by our words. Remember that enhancing the quality of an important kind of information—that what I am doing matters—is precisely the purpose of the transformative language of ongoing regard.

When we practice this noncharacterizing, nonattributing form of communication, it inevitably ends up sounding more sincere, more real, more original. If our appreciation or admiration is attributive, it ends up being drawn from our fund of positive adjectives. As practiced speakers or writers of praise, we can get too good at this. It can become too facile. Consider a place where a glib, not-always-sincere, appreciation-as-praise kind of language lives a healthy life, to which we probably all contribute: the written language of letters of recommendation! We say the person is this way and that way; we have a veritable thesaurus of descriptors we draw on to construct these often hyperbolic characterizations of the other.

This is not what we mean by the language of ongoing regard. Ongoing regard is not about praising, stroking, or positively defining a person to herself or to others. We say again: it is about enhancing the quality of a precious kind of information. It is about informing the person about *our* experience of him or her.

Checkpoint: your nonattributiveness. Take a look, finally, at what you wrote down when we asked you to express an appreciation or admiration. If it has characterizing elements, try right now to restate it, in speech, in a nonattributive fashion. Try to say it aloud as if the person were there with you. (We realize this could create an odd moment on a bus or airplane, but who knows: the person sitting next to you may be quite moved.)

If you take us up on this last invitation, you may find what people we work with tend to find. These communications are inevitably less smooth, more halting, more originally created right there on the spot. They have none of the canned quality of attributive praise. They are fresh. They are more intimate, in a sense, because they are about you, the speaker, revealing something personal about yourself, rather than you assuming you can reveal something about the other. For all these reasons, the result for the listener, and perhaps for you too, is inevitably more powerful.

From the Language of Prizes and Praising to the Language of Ongoing Regard.

Language of Prizes and Praising	Language of Ongoing Regard
• Creates winners and losers; draws energy *out* of the system	• Distributes precious information that one's actions have significance; infuses energy *into* the system
• Frequently communicated indirectly; said *about* person and not directly *to* him or her	• Communicates appreciation or admiration directly to the person
• Usually, global statements giving little if any information about what the speaker is valuing	• Communicates *specific* information to the person about the speaker's personal experience of appreciation or admiration
• Often characterizes the other person	• *Nonattributive;* characterizes the speaker's experience, and not the person being appreciated
• Frequently formulaic; glib	• Sincere and authentic; more halting, freshly made
• Nontransformational	• Transformational potential for both the speaker and the person being regarded

Direct, Specific, Nonattributive: Three Enhancers of the Quality of Information

Being direct, specific, and nonattributive are three features that make the language of ongoing regard more powerful and less subject to formulaic insincerity. The fifth language is about creating a precious kind of information: the news that we ourselves are the difference. Regularly producing this information is like pumping oxygen into the system. It is the support that enables us to stay with the challenge of surfacing our inner contradictions and exploring our questionable Big Assumptions. It is the first line of practice for maintaining the new technology. In Chapter Nine we return to this language and discuss how we can carry on its work.

Chapter Six

From the Language of Rules and Policies to the Language of Public Agreement

"So, good morning to each of you, and we'd like to begin by extending our congratulations! We understand there were a flood of applications and a very deliberate process before your organization selected each of you to be pioneer participants in this exciting process, the creation of your organization's own 'EPCOT'—an experimental prototype company of tomorrow!"

So begins a simulation activity, a little game in which we have, by now, invited many hundreds of professionals to participate. (Depending on the group we are working with, we can sometimes tailor the particular "EPCOT" to be an "experimental prototype college of tomorrow," or "court of tomorrow," or "clinic of tomorrow.") We go on to "remind" the group that their prospective opportunity is to reinvent the way their profession does business; that they were selected to create, in the years ahead, a real-life laboratory to produce learnings that may redesign work and delivery of service in their profession in the twenty-first century.

We next remind them that their new organization will open its doors in three months, that they can expect to be working with each other for at least the next several years, and that no one in the room knows anyone else yet, whether by reputation or previous interaction.

Our last reminder is that they knew when they applied that the only predetermined dimension of their new organizational form is that they are entering a "flat" organization—that is, the professional staff are all to be of equal rank and have equal power and equal say. They may choose to establish temporary "local hierarchies" for the purposes of accomplishing a particular task or running a particular function, but this authority is conferred by the group to a temporary role and does not permanently reside in given persons. Thus they are all leaders and all followers. John may be Mary's boss relative to one project; but a month later, or simultaneously, with regard to a parallel project, their roles could as easily be reversed. (Although the flat organization actually is a popular feature of current discussion about work in the new century, we make it a game condition for much the same reason as the "you don't know each other yet" condition. It simplifies the simulated world by removing two features of normal work relations that greatly constrain thinking about new ways of operating: previous history with colleagues, and subordinates' deference to their bosses' authority.)

Now that they know who they are in this simulation, it is time to let them know who we are, and why we have gathered them together three months before day one in the life of their new organization.

"Of all the things," we tell them from our facilitator's role, "that are special and unique about this moment, we direct your attention to this one: among this group of coworkers, at this moment, there is not yet a single troubled relationship, not a single harbored resentment, not a single shared piece of depreciative gossip. But let's face it: this won't last. Once you begin working together, in spite of your best intentions, often while pursuing even your most commendable goals and commitments, you are going to get into hassles, annoy each other, and step on each other's toes. It's an inevitable feature of work life, even in high-morale, high-performing organizations. But at this moment there is not a single such difficulty—because you have not yet started working together.

"The sponsors of this EPCOT are aware that troubled relationships among coworkers—and the usual things people do with the hurt, angry, or scared feelings they engender—are poisons in the well of work. No matter how solidly the well is built—however inspirational the organization's stated goals, however brilliant the public strategies and procedures for accomplishing them, however generous the company's employee supports and benefits—snagged personal relationships and the conduct that sustains them poison the water and make work life sick. Therefore your sponsors thought it might be prudent to take advantage of this rare moment, before anyone has gotten on anyone's nerves, to see if there isn't some way, ahead of time, to get an antidote into the well. That's where we come in. We've been asked if we might try to help the group create such an antidote."

Developing a Public Agreement: A Collective Route to a First-Column Commitment

Facilitator: Now, our idea is that the route to such antidotes lies in an unpracticed language in professional life, what we call the language of public agreement [which is as different from rules and personnel policies as the language of ongoing regard is different from stroking and praising].

In order to give you a taste of what we mean by a language of public agreement, let's see if together we can come up with even a single agreement about how you would want colleagues in this group to handle things, once this new organization gets started, if they find themselves out of sorts with you. Let's say they are significantly enough bothered in some way with you that this snag has now come to be a fundamental way they experience their relationship with you. What would you want them to do about it? Let's just hear some of your nominations or proposals, and then we'll see if we can agree about any of it.

Participant 1: I'd want them to come to me about it.

Facilitator: Come to you?

Participant 1: Yes, don't be going around talking to everybody else about it, running me down behind my back. If you've got a problem with me, come to me.

Participant 2: Yes. Come to me soon. Don't let it fester.

Participant 3: Not just soon. Come to me first.

Participant 4: Well, I'm not so sure about the "soon" part. I don't want our prototype college of the future to end up being "Whiny U." It might be better if the person would sleep on it for a while, and make sure it's not something that's going to go away on its own before they come bothering me about it. I don't really want everyone at my door the moment after they're ticked off. They might just be having a bad day, and it could all look a lot different tomorrow. So the more I think about it, I'm not a supporter of "soon." But I am a supporter of "come to me first." Take a while to think it over, take as long as you want. But if you are going to talk to someone about it, the person you should talk to first is me.

Participant 5: Yes, I agree. But I'd also want the person to come in a constructive frame of mind. Not just to attack, or to dump, but to talk about how things can get better.

Participant 4: But you do want them to come to you first?

Participant 5: Yes, I do.

Facilitator: Well, we're not suggesting we've come to any real agreement yet, but there does seem to be a lot of consensus around the come-to-me-first part. Let's just check. How may people feel that this is a feature of the agreement they want others to make if they have a problem with you?

[Anywhere from 85 to 95 percent of the hands always go up. Interestingly, we have never done this and *not* had "come to me first" be the emergent favorite for this agreement.]

Facilitator: OK, we haven't all agreed yet, but that's a pretty impressive show of hands. Now we want to remind you: if you make this agreement you are not only saying you want others to come to you first if they are significantly 'snagged' with you, but you also agree that if you are snagged with someone, you too will go to the person first. Now, do you still want to make this agreement?

[Most people say they do, but usually someone comes up with something like this:]

Participant 3: Well, wait a minute. To be honest—if I'm really going to take this seriously and pretend this is a real situation—I'm not sure I want to be bound to go to 'you' first. I'm the kind of person who needs to think out loud, in conversation with someone else. I'd want to go to a friend and say, "Check this out. Here's what Rick did. I'm really steamed. Do you think I'm off base here, or what? Am I overreacting, or is he out of line?" I wouldn't want to bar myself from that kind of conversation. Besides, it could end up changing my angry feelings about Rick and saving him a whole come-to-me conversation!

The Default Mode: Business Behind the Back

Participant 1: Well, I agree with you. I don't think there'd be anything wrong with that kind of conversation. It's a lot different than the kind of talk I was thinking about. That would be for a reality check. I'm in favor of that. But the thing I don't want is what usually does go on: the talking behind people's back, the gossiping, the spreading bad jazz, running people down.

Participant 4: All the usual.

Participant 2: So maybe we should say the agreement is that you should come to me first, or, if you go to another, it should only be in the spirit of checking yourself out, not in the spirit of running the other person down.

Participant 4: Yes.

Participant 3: Yes.

Participant 6: But let's be real. I worry that if we allow that exception, we'll really end up opening the door we are trying to close, because you know as well as I do that when you are talking with a friend and when you are upset it is easy for your friend to take your side and for the conversation to end up being less about a reality check and more about running the other person down.

Participant 4: Well, that's true. It is hard work when someone comes to you like that. Maybe what we should have is a designated "reality check person," a rotating ombudsman, and this is the only other person you can go to, if you don't "come to me first."

[Now, depending on how much time we have, and how long we let this go on, some form of a come-to-me-first agreement, however simple or loaded with qualifications, gets made. This by itself is notable: all groups spontaneously create a come-to-me-first agreement. Yet when we ask if anyone has ever worked in a setting that practiced such a policy, no one says they have. Everyone knows that this behind-the-back, depreciative form of language is corrosive and unprofessional, yet everyone concedes they are a party to it:]

Participant 4: Well, this is just what organizational life is like. I'm not sure you can really do anything about it.

Facilitator: Well, maybe not, but is this why you volunteered to create a brand new prototype organization—to just begin by accepting as inevitable a condition you all agree is poisonous? [Laughter and groans are the usual response to this taunt.]

Participant 4: Well, all right. You want us to keep taking this as real. But then *you* have to be real, too. I don't believe just because we make a come-to-me-first agreement today, people are going to stop talking behind one another's back once we actually do start working together.

The Value of Public Agreements: Not to Prevent Violations But to Create Them

Facilitator: Thank you. Fair enough. Actually, we agree with you. Just because you make this agreement today does *not* mean there will be an end to running people down behind their backs— which brings us quite naturally to the question of what we think is the purpose of a language of public agreement. What if we were to tell you we do not think the value of shared agreements is to *prevent* violations but to *create* them? [This usually leads to an attentive if bewildered silence.] To clarify what we mean, we can ask you another question. Assume you've made this agreement and we wind the clock forward several months into the life of your new organization. Who do you imagine actually has the toughest time keeping this agreement?

Participant 3: The person who's really ticked off at someone he doesn't want to "go to first." [Laughter]

Participant 1: Yeah, someone who'd really rather blow off steam than go talk to the person.

Participant 4: Yes, and that someone, I'll be honest, could just as easily be me. [Laughter] "We're pretending these agreements won't get kept because of a few bad apples, but let's face it: any of us could be the reason we're saying normal life doesn't keep these agreements.

Facilitator: OK. But that's how we may or may not have a tough time breaking the agreement. Let's try something. Would someone volunteer to be a coworker of mine? [Luke volunteers.] OK, thanks Luke. Now, let's pretend there's no one else around but you and me. We're sitting in a private office. We're old running buddies now. Our kids play together. Our families go out to eat together. So the next thing I say to you is: "Say, Luke, can you believe this Ann Marie?! From one meeting to the next, I never know who she's going to set up next. Did you see the way she ran over Hal? Unbelievable, right? She has this sweet smile and soft voice, and she says these incredibly destructive things. I couldn't believe the way she just cut you off this morning. That must burn you too, eh?" [We signal to Luke that it's his turn to reply.]

Luke: Errr—yeah. I wasn't too happy about that. Uhh. Whatever. . . . [Laughter]

Facilitator: Yeah, unbelievable. What do you think her problem is anyway, old buddy. . . ?

Luke: Err, well, who knows. Uhh, I mean—

Facilitator: Time out, Luke. So, how well do you think you're doing keeping our public agreement?

Luke: Not too good. [Shakes his head, laughs; usually the rest of the group joins him in laughing.] Let's try it again.

Facilitator: Great! [Repeats] . . . the way she just cut you off this morning. That must burn you, too, huh?

Luke: Actually, Bob, I'm not really comfortable having that kind of conversation with you. Umm, remember that agreement we made back at the summer retreat? [Laughter from group] I don't want to get drawn into this. I'm still your buddy and everything, but if you've got a problem with Ann Marie, I think we agreed you should take it to her. And I'm looking forward to our families getting together soon for dinner. [Laughter and raucous applause from the admiring group]

The person in Luke's position is our candidate for who may have the toughest job keeping this agreement (although both Luke and Bob have opportunities, as we'll see, to bring our new technology to bear on their present situation). When people initially propose the come-to-me-first agreement, they are usually imagining themselves as the one other is going to come to. Then we invite them to consider that it also means they could be the annoyed person who has to resist talking about others behind their backs and has to come to *them* first.

But the role that is still not thought about, and the one that may make or break the viability of this public agreement, might not be the "tickee" or the "ticker" but the third party. It can be an enormously uncomfortable position in which to find oneself, especially with a close friend whose very words are not merely delivering information but seeking a connection. How do we summon the wherewithal essentially to decline to participate in the very form of language our friend has framed? Where can we look for the resources to do so?

The Work of the Sixth Language: From Relying on Individual Integrity Toward Creating Greater Organizational Integrity

In a group that has no public agreements about such conduct, the only place people have to look for these resources is to the preexisting nature of their own private principles. In such a group, were Bob to have his words responded to in the fashion of Luke's second reply, he would certainly feel some surprise, and possibly some annoyance or hurt at being rebuffed by his friend. But it is also possible that at least some part of him might experience Luke's reply as an expression of Luke's integrity, as well. However much he may admire this, what he is experiencing is Luke's private integrity, which he has no hand in creating and in which he can take no personal pride.

If every organization were filled with many such Lukes, all possessed of their own preexisting integrity, organizational life might be less in need of an antidote to the poisons of back-stabbing communication. But most organizations are not overrun with such people. Even if they were, these people's actions and reactions would continue to be an expression only of their individual private integrity. Leaders and their organizations will always need to draw on, and benefit from, the private, preexisting integrity of individual members. But the ongoing health of our organizations actually depends on leaders' abilities to foster processes that enhance the possibility of collectively experienced, public, *organizational* integrity.

In a group whose leaders have fashioned a language for public agreement—and whose members have used it to create, for example, a come-to-me-first agreement—there is a different answer to the questions "How do we (or Luke) summon the wherewithal to decline to participate in the kind of conversation our coworker friend has framed? Where can we look for the resources to do so?" In this case, Luke has a powerful aid to extricating himself from his difficult predicament. "Remember that agreement we made?" he says.

With words like these, he not merely summons the force of his own private convictions but invokes a collectively created agreement. He is no longer required to oppose his friend with some idea he holds but his friend does not. Rather, he calls upon the organizational memory that public agreements create to remind his friend of an idea they both agreed to hold. Responded to in the fashion of Luke's second reply, Bob might still feel the same initial hurt or annoyance at his friend's refusal. He might still feel some admiration for his friend's integrity.

But in this second case, he has the added opportunity to experience his *own* integrity as well. He himself had a hand in creating the agreement that leads to the boundary his friend draws. As he moves back to the proper side of this boundary, he is less likely to feel only that some individual person has put him in his place. What he's more likely to feel is that he is being moved by his organization's integrity, an integrity he himself has had a hand in creating.

The Organizational Default Mode: Disintegrity

The experience of being acted upon by our organization's *dis*integrity—its forms of unfairness, inattentiveness, and ineffectiveness—is all too common to contemporary work life, widely accepted as standard operating procedure, and a breeder of the cynicism that is today taken for sophistication. The much rarer experience—that I am part of an organization that actually has the capacity to move against the still-existent current of unfairness, inattentiveness, and ineffectiveness—has exactly the opposite effect. It breeds self-respect, renewed commitment to the place where I work, and a feeling of expansiveness.

The ongoing practice of a language of public agreement is a route to nurturing a direct experience of organizational integrity. But it is important to notice that this does not come about through some naïve belief that because everyone holds hands and agrees to something, it removes forever after, like a magic wand, all offending behavior. Not at all. Remember way back in Chapter One that we did not develop a language of commitment by ignoring or turning away from the language of complaining, but rather by turning directly toward it, and creating a context that led us to the language of commitment. In a somewhat similar way, we do not think of the purpose of public agreements as preventing violations but creating them. We fully expect the Bobs of the world to violate the "come to me first" agreement. But notice that it is only because of the existence of a public agreement that his words to Luke about Ann Marie do in fact constitute a violation.

Another way to put this counterintuitive idea is this: *without agreements, there can be no violations.* There can be private objection, certainly. People can feel personal outrage at the acts of others in organizational life. ("I can't believe you went over my head and took that to him without talking to me about it! How could you do such a thing?") "How could you do such a thing?" is the voice of personal outrage. But in the absence of publicly shared agreements, an honest reply (though seldom given) could be, "I never agreed I wouldn't."

The outrage continues: "Well, I just assumed I could count on you. I'd never do a thing like that to you, or anyone else. This isn't the way I understood we were working together." The outrage continues, but it is private, personal outrage. A personal bond is damaged. The organization as a whole is damaged. But nothing owned by the organization—nothing of the public life of the organization—has been violated. There is certainly a cost to the quality and future effectiveness of the organization, but there is no public violation because there has never been a public agreement with respect to the principle that the offended party holds dear.

Who is responsible for this damaging cost? In our view, the party responsible is not primarily the person who caused offense, and not the person who took offense. In our view, the parties primarily responsible are the leaders of the organization who have failed to help it create those public agreements that are available to be made. Without these living organizational structures, there is no way for any offending action or inaction to show up on the public body of the organization as a violation. It is always only a matter of private objection.

So what is the benefit of creating public violations as opposed to private objections (the first outcome of the sixth language)? The ancient Greeks evaluated a society by its practice or neglect of a set of civic virtues, of which one of the most prized was the capacity for collectively experienced outrage, the capacity to summon a shared sense of righteous indignation. We may feel less a part of a cohesive society today not so much because of all the outrageous behavior we see reported in our media but because we are deprived of an accompanying sense of collective offense in response to the outrageous behavior.

Behavior has to become particularly egregious—parents leaving their two-year-old in the care of his five-year-old sibling so the parents can vacation in the Bahamas—for us to experience even a flickering pulse of collective indignation. We are so hungry for the sense of any shared experience that it has become amusing for forty thousand people at sporting events to participate in "the wave," a perfectly empty public agreement. But at least there we all are, for a brief moment, on the same page (even if there is nothing whatever written on the page!).

Leaders have the opportunity to get something written on that page. But how might they do it? The commonly preferred alternative to the "decaying fabric of community life" is some religious or political ideology's presumption of being able by itself to write the words upon the page, or direct us to words written long ago, the proper interpretation of which this new Deliverer claims to possess. The language of public agreement is not a vehicle for leaders to give the troops their marching orders; nor is it meant to create a process to cast out sinners. Rather it is a vehicle for responsible people to collectively imagine a public life they simultaneously know they would prefer and know they will, at times, fall short of. In order for this straw of falling short to be turned into the gold of organizational and individual learning, there needs to exist a context that turns private objection into public violation. This is the first purpose of the sixth language, one of shared agreements.

So, granting that agreements such as the come-to-me-first agreement do not magically banish corrosive, dysfunctional ways of handling our snagged relationships with our coworkers, what are the specific opportunities an ongoing language of public agreement creates? The two principal outcomes of a language of public agreement are (1) the experience of organizational integrity (in contrast to ordinary experiences of organizational unfairness, inattentiveness, or ineffectiveness, which create the demoralizing and enervating experience of disintegrity); and (2) the use of violations as a resource for surfacing further inner contradictions for our learning (in contrast to treating violations as the professional equivalent of shameful sin). We briefly elaborate on each of these as a way of concluding this introduction to our sixth language, and remind you that we return to consideration of how to further pursue the practice of this, and every, language in Chapters Eight and Nine.

The Public Work of the Sixth Language: Toward More Organizational Integrity

As we said, when Luke responds to his temporarily back-biting friend, Bob, by invoking not merely his personal discomfort at being a participant in this conversation but also the shared agreement he and Bob took part in making, he is helped out of his awkward social position and at the same time he uses the agreement to enhance both his own and (potentially) Bob's experience of organizational integrity. Luke experiences his access to a living organizational mechanism, by which he is able to reset a boundary his friend has violated. He can experience not simply himself but also his organization as more effective, fairer, and more attentive in response to a situation that otherwise adds a little poison to the well of work.

Similarly, Bob has the opportunity to experience effective, fair, attentive forces at work in his own organization, as well; forces he helped create; forces that he now sees from experience have the strength to gently pick him up and return him to the proper side of the boundary he has crossed. Neither person has any of these experiences if, in fact, Bob does not violate the agreement. So his violation—where a living language of public agreement exists—is actually a potential resource, rather than a sign that the agreements are in practice meaningless. The life of an agreement merely begins with its original ratification; its real strength and vitality are demonstrated by use in response to the inevitable violations that its presence creates.

Although shared agreements certainly do not prevent violations, injecting more boundary-restoring moves like Luke's into organizational life may actually over time reduce the number of violations. Bob is less likely to keep bringing the same depreciative conversation about Ann Marie (or anyone?) to Luke. To the extent others respond to him as Luke has done (Bob may well unconsciously test for the weak link in this boundary, as he hunts for a "new Luke"), he may bring this kind of conversation less often to anyone. To some extent, then, using a public agreement (rather than the agreement itself) may serve as a counterforce against the inevitable, ongoing tide of organizational disintegrity. Using the agreements may thus alter organizational life to some extent by controlling or reducing the Bob-type behavior.

In most of the literature on organizational learning, this reduction of dysfunctional behavior, should it occur, would itself be taken as a sign of learning. Such a definition of learning grows out of a positivist, behavioral-conditioning conception that essentially looks at learning as little more than altered behaviors in response to given stimuli in order to accomplish some aim or goal. The rat that learns to depress a lever to gain a food pellet is a classic example. As should be clear by now, our interest is in transformational learning. Our orientation to learning, at its origins, is more epistemological than behavioral. We are interested in changes of behavior that rise out of changes in knowing.

We don't believe the rat itself has actually been transformed for "learning" to depress a lever. We suspect that, if returned to its normal organizational life so to speak, the rat has developed no greater capacity to contribute to its community. A Bob who actually begins to understand himself differently (and Ann Marie, and Luke, too) has a lot more to bring to his organization than a Bob who has merely been conditioned to stop pressing the backbiting lever because he has "learned" that he will not gain the pellet of an approving colleague.

The Internal Work of the Sixth Language: Rebooting the New Technology

This brings us to the second possibility created by a language of shared agreement. Such a context has the promise of creating more of the experience of organizational integrity; it can also be a producer of just those inner contradictions that, we have already seen (in Chapter Three), are a rich resource for transformational learning. As Chapter Nine shows, when we consider how to work further with this language, we do not suggest that our violations be viewed with self-recrimination but instead with a particular kind of curiosity. We believe they should be taken not to an organization's courtroom but to its classroom. We believe we should take responsibility for them, but in the manner of a learner, not a penitent.

Let's go back to Bob and Luke. Bob violated an agreement he himself made when he took his problem with Ann Marie to Luke and proceeded not to explore self-critically his own reaction but to try to win Luke's assent to his negative characterization of Ann Marie. Similarly, Luke (in his first rendition) violated the same agreement when he let himself become part of this conversation. Now, does this necessarily mean that Bob or Luke was insincere or hypocritical when he made the agreement? Certainly not. We have already demonstrated (in Chapters One and Two) that everyone of us, with little difficulty, can identify a commitment we simultaneously and genuinely affirm yet undermine by our own actions or inactions. We could all be Bob or Luke.

It's one thing if a person never really sincerely agrees to the agreement. In that case, the most important learning may involve looking more openly at the disjunction between, on the one hand, a group that is gradually (through a series of agreements) becoming more explicit in its definition of who and how it wants to be and, on the other, a particular member who is coming to see that he cannot sincerely sign on to this emerging definition. This may be a much more informative and self-evident context for a group and the member to decide to part ways than what most organizations usually provide. People leave or are required to leave organizations every day—usually with very little experience of the organization's integrity on anyone's part. A departure brought about because the organization has better defined how it wants to operate, and what it stands for (a collective column-one commitment, in the language of earlier chapters), can offer everyone (even the person who is leaving because he is not a good match with this clearer definition) a greater sense of the organization's integrity.

But in most cases violations arise out of a far more interesting and complicated source. Rather than having entered the agreement insincerely, the person may be genuinely committed to the agreement and its purpose (what we called column one in Chapter One)—and, like Bob or Luke, still violate the agreement (column two, in Chapter Two).

What would it mean for either of them to take a curious and learning-oriented (as opposed to self-recriminating and penitential) stance toward their violation? A quick review of the earlier chapters of this book should lead to a good answer to this question. If they take a self-recriminating and penitential stance toward their column-two behaviors (the usual form of responsibility) it would lead to what we have called New Year's Resolutions—promises, no matter how well intended, to shape up, promises that predictably have very little power or effect.

On the other hand, if they use their column-two behaviors as a portal to some other kinds of commitment they hold, they may be able to use the language of public agreement to reboot the new learning technology, to create a roomier space for self-reflection that may actually lead to changes in behavior resulting from changes in knowing.

From the Language of Rules and Policies to the Language of Public Agreement.

Language of Rules and Policies	Language of Public Agreement
• Customary	• Exceedingly rare, without leaderly intention
• Intended to create order (from the top down, or the outside in)	• Intended to create organizational integrity (institutional fairness, attentiveness, and competence) from within
• Institutionalized in written manuals or through implicit norms, with little or no discussion of the meaning of the rules and policies, and no experience of owning them or assenting to them	• Shared understanding of their meaning and an experience of co-owning them and assenting to them
• Frequently discussed only after there is a violation	• Discussed and created before violation to establish a shared understanding and reference point in order to enhance personal and organizational learning when there is a violation
• Violations are ignored or treated privately and as a matter of adjudication for problem elimination	• Violations are treatable publicly as a resource for personal and organizational learning, by creating observable contradictions
• Multiple interpretations frequently exist, and people tend to be unaware of this	• Common understanding of the agreements themselves and their purpose
• Creates a social vehicle for leaders or authorities to correct boundary transgressions	• Creates a social vehicle for peers to correct boundary transgressions
• "Corrected" individuals experience the organization's ability to control behavior—an ability they have no part in creating	• "Corrected" individuals experience the organization's integrity, which they themselves have a hand in creating
• Nontransformational; shapes behavior, not new meanings	• Transformational for both the individual and the organization

A Case of Knowing

Let's close this chapter with an example of a real case that reminds us of the first-rendition Luke. Not long ago, we worked with a fellow who was living exactly Luke's predicament. He was genuinely committed to direct communication among colleagues in problematic relationships and not being a third party to depreciative conversation. Yet he was honest enough to admit that he quite frequently participated as a third party in exactly these kinds of conversations.

Given the opportunity to generate a hidden third-column commitment out of these undermining behaviors (as we did in Chapter Three), he said something like this:

> What would I be afraid of were I to do otherwise? Hmmm, well, I think if I didn't respond as I do to the many people who love to come to me and tell me about their difficulties with this person or that person, uh, I'd feel like I had given up one of the things that make me feel important and special at work, to tell you the truth. This is something I'm very good at, you see. And I do like being the person people feel comfortable bringing these things to! So, I guess, putting this in your terms, it would be kind of, "I am committed to feeling special and important at work by being the person people like to come to with their gossip and complaints."

His exploration of his violation of a shared come-to-me-first agreement has led him to construct an internal contradiction: "I am genuinely committed to direct communication between snagged coworkers (and not being drawn in as a third party); and I am also committed to feeling special and important at work by being called upon to hear people's gossip and complaints." This fellow has now used the experience of his violation to reboot the new technology. He has been able to move from a view of the violation itself to a view of the bigger immune system he creates to continuously manufacture nonchange.

He has also now identified a wonderful problem! It is just the sort of problem he would do well not to solve too quickly, but to stay with for purposes of seeing how it might solve him, as we put it. What is more, the tension in this contradiction is interpersonal, social, and organizational as much as internal because it puts him in difficulty with a shared public agreement. As we will see in

Chapter Nine, this need not make matters worse but actually better, since there are more reasons (and resources) for him to stay engaged in the contradiction.

As we discussed in Chapter Three, it is common for organizations to conspire with the part of us that wants to make internal contradictions invisible. But if the internal contradiction also puts us at odds with public agreements, the organization is not so likely to look the other way. On the contrary, it will probably look right at us. Instead of colluding with the part of us that wants to skip school, it has the opportunity to become itself a good teacher, engaging the phenomenon with genuine curiosity, and asking the good question, "What's up?"

Chapter Seven

From the Language of Constructive Criticism to the Language of Deconstructive Criticism

You'll notice we've saved the subject of conflict for our seventh and last language. Ironically, when we are invited into organizations, or departments, or work teams, often the very first thing people want to get into is conflict. "We've got a lot of issues here, and no good way to deal with them. You're psychologists. Perhaps you can help us work this stuff out." Or: "We'll fight. You referee." We routinely decline these invitations, suggesting we need to work up to productive approaches to conflict. We postpone that language— just as we have done here.

This is not because we are squeamish about confrontation or angry communication. It is not because we believe consultants need to ease in to troubled waters only gradually and indirectly. It is not because we believe people are so fragile they need to be protected from the discomfort of another's unfavorable view of their behavior.

So why do we come to conflict later rather than sooner? Something we keep in mind in our work with groups is that we want to take steps—from the very first day—toward the goal of putting ourselves out of business, toward the group's no longer having a need for us. We want our ways of working with others to decrease rather than increase their dependency on us. Accordingly, we want the group, rather than ourselves, to be the keeper of the competence to exercise a given language. If a group is not prepared, for example, to practice a language of ongoing regard or personal responsibility, it is not sufficient for us to be the source of direct, specific, and nonattributive admiration and appreciation, or for us to be the sole holders of the responsibility. We simply do not succeed in the practice of that language if it is only convened and sustained by us. Why? As soon as we withdrew, the language collapses; the language goes to sleep.

Thus our insistence on developing a group's capacity to practice the other languages first before we turn to conflict arises less from an overly soft or sweet disposition and more from our stern judgment that most groups initially lack the collective competence to practice a conflict-oriented language in a productive, learning-oriented fashion. (When one group challenged our refusal to begin at the level of intragroup conflict, we made this assumption behind our refusal explicit and invited them to test it with us if they liked. They were a group of individually highly skilled persons, but they soon discovered that collectively they were not ready to wade into these waters.)

Accordingly, if our purposes are aimed not at technical, temporary, externally mediated fixes but instead at developing an organization's ongoing internal capacity to transform conflict into an opportunity for group and individual learning, then we believe our proper focus is on the group's development of this competence rather than on our effectively refereeing the safest, fairest possible fight. Because we believe the practice of productive conflict is a high art, we don't start here. We think a group needs time, not to summon its courage or to develop a thicker skin but to accomplish a necessary set of prior learnings.

It may be intuitively obvious that there is a better chance for productive expressions of conflict where there is also ongoing regard; where people take responsibility for their own hand in the matter and not merely blame others; where people are aware of how their own big assumptions and commitments toward self-protection may contribute to the conflictual situations; where people have made prior public agreements, perhaps including agreements about how to handle conflict. But in addition, we may need to reconsider what we even think productive expressions of conflict sound like in the first place.

Most people imagine something like the brave exchange of bombshells, of people finally telling it like it is. But a language of difficult truths, however temporarily air clearing it may be to enunciate them, however brave it may be to stay present to hear them, does not necessarily lead to transformational learning. We may need first to consider whether what we are telling is how it *is*—the truth at last to set us free—or how it *seems* to us. Without a language first designed around sustaining this crucial distinction, everything that follows may be guaranteed to reproduce rather than reconstruct the present conflict.

The Default Modes: Destructive or Constructive Criticism

Let's consider a simple version of conflictual communication in order to distinguish our way of thinking about a learning-oriented approach to conflict from those we carry around in our heads or find in the current literature. Consider the situation of your giving critical feedback to a colleague or subordinate. The conflict, from your point of view, is between the quality of your colleague's or subordinate's performance and the quality you desire.

Now for a quick exercise. Think back to a recent time when you were in a situation in which you had to give another person negative feedback. This may be a situation where you knew you needed to talk to the other person but didn't, or one you are currently in and considering how to handle. At the top of a sheet of paper, write "Here's the situation that prompted the conversation:" or similar language (as in Notepad 1 below). Take a couple of minutes to describe in writing the situation that prompted the conversation. Then, on the same sheet of paper, add the other prompts seen in Notepad 1 and write your responses to them. In doing so, you record (1) what you said (or would have said), (2) what the other person said (or might have said had the conversation occurred), and (3) your feelings before and during the conversation. Also, write down (4) your reactions to how the conversation went (if you had it) and why you think you had those reactions. Finally, if you still remember the time leading up to the conversation, jot down (5) how you were feeling about it beforehand, and why. If you were nervous or anxious, why do you suppose you felt that way? If you were eager for the conversation, why might you have been looking forward to having it?

Notepad 1.

1. Here's the situation that prompted the conversation:

2. Here's a rough "verbatim" of the first things I said (or would have said) and the other's real or imagined response:

3. Here's what I was feeling before and during the conversation, and some thoughts about why I might have felt that way:

4. Here are my reactions to the way the conversation went and some thoughts about why I'm reacting that way:

5. Here's what I was feeling before the conversation, and some thoughts about why I might have felt that way:

We'll return to this situation later in this chapter.

In a *New York Times* review of a book by Hendrie Weisinger (Sept. 16, 1990), Daniel Goleman gives us an example of this kind of situation:

> An engineer presented a plan for developing new software to the vice president of his high-technology company. With his team, the engineer waited expectantly, hoping for praise and encouragement; the plan was the result of months of work.
>
> But the reaction from the vice president was harsh: "These specifications are ridiculous," he said. "They haven't a chance of getting past my desk." Then, his voice thick with sarcasm, he added, "How long have you been out of graduate school?"

Now, take a moment to react to this bit of feedback. What do you think of it, and why? On another sheet of paper, reproduce the headings in Notepad 2 below. In writing your responses to what you think of the vice president's feedback and why, be specific about what features of it you see as potentially destructive or risky practice (if you do), and why. Do the same for any of the features you see as potentially constructive (if you do).

Notepad 2.

Feedback (Example of Engineer and Vice President)	
Constructive:	**Destructive:**
•	•
•	•
•	•
•	•
•	•

Starting with your list of constructive and destructive features of the vice president's feedback to the engineer, you can now generate a first-draft list of do's and don'ts about giving feedback. On a new sheet of paper, create the heads and columns of Notepad 3 below. Try to be specific in making entries in the two columns. If, for example, you think it is counterproductive for the vice president to ask, "How long have you been out of graduate school?," you might write, "Don't ridicule" or "Don't ask sarcastic questions" in the *don't* column.

Weisinger, a psychologist at the School of Management at UCLA and author of *The Critical Edge,* assessed the vice president's feedback, just as we've asked you to do. We're guessing you won't be surprised that he sees this as an example of a collection of the most common errors managers make in giving negative feedback. He says, "The worst way to criticize is with a blanket statement like, 'You're really screwing up,' without offering the person some way to do better." His reason: "It leaves the other person feeling helpless and angry." Figure 7.1 is Weisinger's version of the do's and don'ts generated by the example of the vice president's feedback to the engineer.

We're guessing that your list probably shares a number of Weisinger's suggestions. It doesn't surprise us if you have many of them. When asked to stop and think about it, most of us know the basic ingredients for giving feedback skillfully.

Notepad 3.

When Giving Feedback	
Do:	**Don't:**
•	•
•	•
•	•
•	•
•	•

Figure 7.1. One Psychologist's
Assessment of Example of Good and Bad Feedback.

Constructive:	Destructive:
• Specific: The manager says exactly what the person is doing wrong, such as "This is what I like, and why."	• Vague: Offers no specifics, but makes a blanket condemnation, such as, "That was a lousy job."
• Supportive: Gives the sense that the criticism is meant to help the person do better.	• Blames the person: Attributes the problem to personality or some other unchangeable trait.
• Problem solving: Suggests a solution or offers to help to find a way to improve things.	• Threatening: Makes the person feel attacked, such as, "Next time, you're through."
• Timely: Gives the message soon after the problem occurs.	• Pessimistic: Offers no hope for change or suggestion for doing better.

Source: Weisinger, H. *The Critical Edge: How to Criticize up and down Your Organization and Make It Pay Off.* (1990).

Now, if someone does what we would call an "informational" training session, their goal might be to help you put these tips into practice systematically. Surely we have all had the experience of knowing something intellectually but then having a difficult time putting the idea into practice. So, we might be asked to look back at our own feedback or conflict situation and assess the match between what we produced and what advice like Weisinger's might produce. Then we might be asked to identify the gaps and try to produce more effective statements.

After a short while, and with effective feedback from a fellow participant about how we are doing, we probably master these skills. The challenge is then whether we can produce such effective or skillful criticism when we next need to in real time at work. If we stick with it (maybe we go to a refresher workshop, or ask someone we go with to help us), we believe that we surely will succeed in learning how to apply these ideas more consistently and, by doing so, be a proficient deliverer of what Weisinger and most reasonable people consider constructive feedback.

We also believe the following: many a relationship has been damaged and a work setting poisoned by *perfectly delivered* constructive feedback! (Or, as Bill Perry used to say, "The helping hand strikes again!")

If forced to choose between destructive feedback and constructive feedback, we imagine you, like us, would prefer the latter. We are not about to advocate a preference for Weisinger's other column. *But these are not our only choices.* We use this chapter to suggest a conflict-laden language that is as different from constructive conflict as the language of ongoing regard is from praising and prize giving, and the language of public agreement is from rules and policies.

The Unexamined Big Assumption Behind Constructive Criticism

Let's return to Weisinger's perfectly reasonable tips and see if we can infer any undisclosed assumptions that may underlie them. Take another look at Figure 7.1. Consider the content of the two columns, and ask yourself if you can identify any assumptions underlying the suggestions. A question that might help you see an assumption is this: What might we be taking as a given or presuming to be true that makes these tips cohere and sound sensible to us?

Several juicy assumptions seem to us to be inferable, although none of them is acknowledged or made explicit by Weisinger. The first is that the perspective of the feedback giver (let's call him the supervisor)—what he sees and thinks, his feedback—is right, is correct. An accompanying assumption is that there is only one correct answer. When you put these two assumptions together, they amount to this: the supervisor has the one and only correct view of the situation. (We call this "the super vision assumption"; that is, the supervisor has *super* vision.) The corollary of these assumptions is that the person receiving the feedback (let's call him the employee) doesn't have the right answer; his perspective is wrong.

A further assumption seems to be that the supervisor is the one who has, or should have, the lion's share of responsibility in this situation. He is the one presumably prepared to (1) say exactly what the person is doing wrong, (2) give the sense the criticism is meant to help, (3) suggest a solution, and (4) give a timely message. Related to this is the idea that the supervisor is the one who should do the saying, suggesting, and giving, and that the employee's responsibilities are to listen, accept, and receive.

If something like these assumptions is at work underlying these apparently reasonable do's and don'ts, it then follows that the purpose of the criticism is for the supervisor to get the employee to see things correctly; that is, to transfer what is in the supervisor's head (the correct answer) to the employee's head (which is in need of the correct answer). People in education talk about this idea as the transmission model of education, because the activity is all about sending a message to a receiver—just like the computer activity of downloading.

"Come in, Frank. I've been eager to communicate downward to you."

Exploring the Big Assumption

We want to be clear that we are not saying any or all of these assumptions are bad, invalid, or unwarranted. As we've said in Chapter Four, becoming aware of our assumptions does not require us to declare them inaccurate or invalid. Once aware of them, however, we can begin a mindful relationship to the assumptions. We are now in a position to ask some questions: What really is my operating assumption here? What do I think about it? What are some of the costs I may pay for holding it? In what kind of situation? What are some of the benefits? Do I always benefit, or is it circumstance-specific? Perhaps most important, how might I learn whether it's valid?

To explain what we mean, let's focus on the assumption that the vice president has the right answer. This assumption might be valid on those occasions where there is only one correct answer (which, of course, raises the question of whether there is a right answer to the question "Which situations have only one correct answer?"!). The idea of one right and many wrongs makes sense to us if we think about a closed system, like a jigsaw puzzle, with its pieces before us. We know there is only one way the pieces can successfully be joined to form a whole picture. (Even those new "many-in-one" puzzles, which have pictures on both sides of each puzzle piece and can form a number of distinct pictures depending on which side and which pieces you place together, are a form of closed system. Yes, a more complex system than the traditional one-picture puzzle, but still a closed one.)

Whether we are right or wrong in situations of this kind, there is still the issue of open-ended situations with no one right answer, where multiple legitimate viewpoints exist. Here there are a number of legitimate ways to fit the pieces together to form entirely different pictures. Even more complex situations come to mind: there may be an undetermined number of puzzle pieces, or the very act of deciding whether something even is a puzzle piece requires making judgments and engaging in interpretation, or perhaps no one knows what the picture will look like in the end.

In these cases, we cannot simply be right. We can, however, be relatively right. This depends on our accepting that there are multiple legitimate pictures and agreeing to choose to accept a particular one. Right in these instances is relative to the one legitimate picture. So we can be right in these instances if we have, for example, accurate and high-quality data, have a shared frame of reference with our employee for how to interpret those data, and develop a well-reasoned interpretation that accounts for all the important data.

Sometimes our assumption that we're right, even in complex situations, is legitimate. Yet there are surely occasions when that same assumption is not justified. Once we consider both possibilities, we need to acknowledge that we can't simply be sure about our perspective (otherwise, we'd be back to operating out of the assumption that we know the right answer). We may be right about being right, but we may also be wrong. Perhaps we assess the situation based on incomplete data, or perhaps we assume the person is trying to accomplish one thing when she is actually trying to do something else. Maybe this is one of those situations where there is no one correct answer. Maybe our perspective is legitimate (or maybe not), but it isn't *the* truth anymore since we are no longer in the realm of simply one right answer. In this case, it's also possible that our employee has a valid view.

We want to be honest here and say that we chose to focus on the "I'm right" or super-vision assumption because we see it as high up on a top-ten list for conflict conditions that are counterproductive to learning. This particular assumption seals off our learning and, in doing so, maintains its powerful hold on our certainty. Why? Because we have little, if any, reason to check ourselves if we assume we are right. People may be sending us messages communicating that we ought to rethink our position, but if we never doubt our perspective, then it's quite possible that we interpret their signals to mean something else.

Our unchecked assumption that we are right remains intact by our interpreting things out there in a way that is consistent with our being right. If the supervisor assumes he is right, it is likely he holds the assumption we identified earlier that the purpose of the critical conversation is to get the other person to change. He is then primed to interpret everything the employee says or asks that conveys disagreement as evidence of a continued problem: "He's being defensive," or "He can't learn," or "He's stupid." It doesn't occur to the supervisor that his own view may be unclear, or limited, or wrong. Clearly, the supervisor can't learn whether his own view is right under these conditions.

The Vested Interest of "Truth"

Something else we find remarkable about this very powerful assumption is the stranglehold it has on us: as long as we hold our view to be true, we have a vested interest in maintaining the truth of our view. No one willingly gives up the truth.

This vested interest translates into various behaviors. Consider, for example, how we may want to avoid giving someone criticism. If we believe our criticism is true, then it's easy to understand why we would feel badly about telling it to a person. We know that the truth can hurt. We can feel responsible for carrying the truth and in communicating it, and then burdening the other with it.

But consider, instead, how it feels if we enter a conversation with the same person, with the same criticism in mind, but we know we may not be totally right or may even be wrong. Suddenly we shift from thinking about kind or clever ways to help the person see it our way (someone once told us that he knew he had gotten reviewed by an experienced, skillful manager when he didn't realize until hours after their exchange that he'd even been given negative feedback!) to thinking about trying to understand what's been happening and whether our criticism is warranted. We become explorers, tentative with our meanings, and open to changing them when we discover new vantage points or information.

Additional costs may be incurred by the receivers of our truths and by our need to be right. Once we establish our meaning as the standard and norm against which we evaluate other people, we essentially hold them to our personal preferences (which are sometimes noble and fair, and other times not).

A high price is paid by the less-powerful recipients when we hold them accountable to our preferences. Consider the situation where as managers we give a subordinate the bad news that she screwed up with the task we delegated to her. We prepare our part of the meeting, taking care to be fair that we are specific about the problems we see and being sensitive to present our materials to minimize her defensiveness and maximize her sense that we want to help. Will this subordinate directly question our judgment? Or question the quality of the data we have based our judgment on? Probably not. She will probably feel obligated to do as we tell her.

She's paid a price, and so have we. Our organization eventually pays a price as well, since our tacit message to her (and everyone who can read the politics of power) is to not think or make judgments on her own, but to follow the directions and directives of her supervisor.

Now let's get back to your own earlier exercise: your account of a negative feedback experience. As you've no doubt expected, we wonder whether you see the "I'm right" assumption operating in your opening words of the conflictual dialogue, though we can well imagine that our having gone on at length about the potential problems of holding this assumption may lead you to hope you're not one of those people who do.

But actually there's nothing to be ashamed of. The fact is, you are in excellent and plentiful company; in our experience working with top executives, judges, doctors, psychologists, school heads, and university administrators, the "I'm right" assumption is one of the most popular among people in leadership positions. Second, we want to remind you that often the things about which we feel sheepish, even embarrassed, aren't expressions of our genetic makeup, or static personality traits, but expressions of other, potentially mutable commitments and assumptions we hold.

Toward a Third Alternative: Deconstructive Criticism

So what are we suggesting is a third alternative to destructive and constructive criticism? What is the alternative to demeaning, depreciative, punishing communication on the one hand, intended to tear a person down, and timely, sympathetic, supportive, explicit, instructive, and problem-solving communication on the other, intended to build the person up? As Figure 7.2 indicates, behind the apparent virtue of constructive criticism there lies a collection of barriers to learning that can be overcome by stepping back not from our negative evaluations but from a truth-claiming relationship to our negative judgments. We call this stance a deconstructive one because its central intention is neither to tear down nor build up but instead disassemble, and the object of attention is not first of all the other but our own evaluation or judgment. The

Figure 7.2. Two Approaches
to Conflict-Laden Communication.

Attribute	Constructive Communication for Informative Behavioral Change	Deconstructive Communication for Transformative Learning
The effective communicator . . .	Gets the person to change	Creates a context for learning
Primary theater of activity	External: the actions or inactions of the other person	Internal: the meanings and assumptions of both parties
Who is at risk of learning?	Only the other person—and even then, only learning about what the communicator thinks or wants for the other	Both parties
How the other is seen	As a misbehaver, doer of actions	As a whole meaning maker or system whose actions or choices express some general belief, conviction, principle, theory
Who has the truth of the situation?	Communicator knows the truth	Neither necessarily; perhaps either, both, or neither
Who doesn't get it?	Other: "You are lost, missing something, overlooking, forgetting, never knew something which I am trying to find the kindest, most effective way of filling you in on"; "teaching" stance vs. inquirer's stance	Communicator: "I see what you are doing or not doing and, given my take, I don't get it"; genuine report of puzzlement (vs. criticism) and inquiry into how this can make sense
The essence of conflict is contradiction, and contradiction is . . .	A management problem in need of resolution	A rich resource for individual and organizational learning

Figure 7.2. Two Approaches
to Conflict-Laden Communication, Cont'd.

Attribute	Constructive Communication for Informative Behavioral Change	Deconstructive Communication for Transformative Learning
Basic stances	"I'm right" or "You're wrong (but you'll get defensive, so . . .); how do I tell you the bad news? how do I get you to change?"	Respect for self ("I have a take on this and it *does* lead me to think you are 'wrong' here, but . . .")
	"Teaching" you	Respect for other ("You are also a whole person with your own take")
	"I'm setting you straight"	Active uncertainty; not paralysis and indecision, but holding of own view tentatively—"Given how I see things I'm puzzled" but seeking clarity, via honest inquiry (we both may change our minds): "Could you set me straight as to how I've got this wrong . . . ?"

conversational arena that sustains this novel approach to difference, disagreement, negative judgment, and critical feedback we call the language of deconstructive conflict.

The New Technology Revisited:
A "Big Assumption" Approach to Outer Contradiction

As it has probably occurred to you by now, the third alternative to conflict amounts to bringing our four-column technology for personal learning into the social, interpersonal, organizational world. By recasting conflict as a form of "outer contradiction" (the social equivalent of the dynamic equilibrium that continuously manufactures nonchange), we are inevitably driven to surfacing for first-time examination the Big Assumptions that hold the equilibrium in place.

An example may provide a quick route into the deconstructive stance. As part of a recent team-building retreat we ran for a group of school administrators, we asked the participants to comment on how they perceived their team on a number of dimensions, such as decision making and conflict. When we got to the dimension of conflict, they told us, "That's actually not one of our problem areas. We rarely disagree, and when we do, it's never a big deal." We have learned that the "no big deal" response to conflict in the workplace can sometimes mean "It's such a big deal that we don't dare touch it." So we saw it as our job—if they were willing—to try to understand what this particular team meant by "no big deal."

With their permission to pursue better understanding of how conflict operates in their team, we invited them into a simple exercise (which, of course, we ask you to participate in now!). We asked them to look at the drawing on the next page and told them we would give them a chance to talk with each other about what they saw.

We were guessing from facial expressions that some people were puzzled about what there was to discuss about this picture, let alone how the picture had anything to do with the topic of conflict. (If you're playing along in this exercise, what do you see?) People began talking. One person said she saw a youngish woman. Others joined in: "Yeah, and she has a small nose." "She's also wearing a necklace and a feathered hat." Other people were saying, "What?" "Where?" "I see an older-looking woman." "Yeah, someone with a large nose." "And she's wearing a scarf around her head."

Several minutes into this exchange, we asked people to do a quick check-in with themselves: "How are you feeling right now?" People's responses varied. Several voiced their puzzlement, reciting some version of "How can they see a different woman? I don't." "Why don't I see it?" Others were also puzzled but disbelieving as well, communicating something like "I don't see this other woman they're all talking about. Are they serious?" Some people indicated that they felt nervous and unsure about what would happen. A number of people described themselves as frustrated: "I can't see her" (meaning, whichever figure eluded their first impression).

We hadn't yet heard from everyone when there was a loud, re-
lieved, "Oh, wait—I see!" Two participants had been talking to each
other, each apparently having seen a different woman. One of them
was able to show the other "where" the other picture of a woman
was. (If you're looking to find the other woman, try this: if you saw
the young woman and are looking for the older one, try turning
her ear into an eye, which will then lead to her nose becoming the
old woman's other eyelash, her chin and jawline into a nose, her
necklace into a mouth, and her neck into a chin. If you saw the
older woman and are looking for the younger one, try turning the
more visible of her two eyes into an ear, the less visible eye into an
eyelash and a side view of a little nose, her nose into a chin and jawline, her mouth into a necklace, and her chin into a neck.)

You may have seen this picture before and know that it comes
from the Gestalt perception psychology of the 1930s. The picture
intentionally invites two interpretations. A trick picture, yes, but
far less tricky than reality itself. The process of both interpreting
the picture and talking about that interpretation in the context of
a group recreates some of the most basic elements of, and assumptions operative during, interpersonal conflict.

Many people, in spite of the fact that there were others who
did not see the same picture they did, never doubted what they
saw. Some of these people were interested in seeing what the other

people were talking about. Of these people, many struggled to get the other picture. They were motivated to keep looking because so many people apparently saw another woman. For many, it was frustrating to have their hardest efforts fail to show another person what they saw.

This kind of experience raises the question of *where* the picture is. We tend to assume that the picture is on the page. (Why else do we tend not to look for another picture once one has been seen?) We also assume that there is just one picture on the page: if twenty copies of the picture are passed out and they all look the same to us, it seems that everyone is getting the same picture, so to speak. (Why else does it come as a surprise to hear people giving answers different from our own?) We assume, then, that what we see is the picture.

Actually the picture is not so much on the page—the page contains a smattering of dark and light patches, lines and blank space—as it is composed in, and by, each of us as a meaning-making organism. We actively make sense of those dark and light patches. Our point is that people create their own reality rather than picking up one that exists out there. Interpersonal problems emerge because our reality isn't another person's reality. Conflict, feedback, and interpersonal disagreement can all be understood as expressions of our human ability to compose meaning—different meanings from another's. Unto itself, having different meanings isn't a problem. We make it a problem if we insist that our meaning is the better one without ever exploring its validity. When we do this, we have turned our meanings into Big Assumptions.

(By the way, after a discussion about people as meaning makers, retreat participants began to paint a more complex picture of themselves as a team than their earlier no-problem rendition. Within a couple of hours, people expressed a toned-down version of "It's such a big deal that we don't dare touch it," and by midmorning they were beginning to talk about some of the issues over which there was significant disagreement.)

Not only are different meanings not necessarily a problem, but if we think back to earlier chapters we see that a central element of the internal languages presented in Part One of this book is the hard work we did to surface and sustain a relationship to the different (contradictory, disagreeing) meanings we ourselves create internally.

Internal contradictions, we suggested, though at times an uncomfortable road to walk, help build the royal road to transformational
learning. *Interpersonal* contradictions, the language of deconstructive
conflict suggests, can further build that road. We do not see conflict,
even ongoing conflict, as necessarily debilitating or dysfunctional
for organizational life. Rather, it is conflict's unproductive use—its
misuse, actually—that is debilitating and dysfunctional.

No leader or leadership team can be expected to banish all
conflict from our midst—though many have tried (with the collu-
sive assistance of the followers), and the familiar result is that the
conflict is driven underground, where it corrodes work life at its
roots. But every leader or leadership team, as a language shaper,
has the opportunity to create a frame for understanding and using
conflict that not only prevents it from undermining the good order
of the organization but actually transforms it into a resource for
individual and organizational learning. This is the ambition and
purpose of the seventh and last language.

Engaging the Seventh Language: Ten Challenges to Our Big Assumption

Engaging this language requires us first to engage our Big Assumptions about conflict itself, including the "I'm right" assumption. In a moment, we are going to consider ten challenges for
deconstructing. They are all directed toward helping us explore
our Big Assumption, to take our meanings and interpretations
apart, to "unthing" them, so that we may reform them whenever
we see the need. Collectively, these challenging propositions remind us of the numerous ways we may be wrong, the point of
which isn't to belittle or berate ourselves. Nor is it to be tough on
ourselves for the sake of being tough. Seeing that we may be wrong
is the yang to the much more accessible and hearty yin of our need
to be (and belief that we are) right.

To try on these ideas less abstractly, we suggest you return to
the opening exercise of this chapter, in which you thought of an
actual conflict situation you are or have been in. You can ground
your reaction to each challenging proposition by letting it perme-
ate the real-life space of your remembered conflict situation. We

don't expect the propositions in Notepad 4 to immediately intrigue or delight you, set off light bulbs, or instantly create a harmonious feeling for you about this heretofore problematic situation. More likely, most of them (starting around number two) are going to evoke forms of impatience, skepticism, or annoyance. On a sheet of paper set up to resemble Notepad 4, record your reactions in the right-hand column opposite each proposition. We welcome, and even hope for, a rich collection of your push-backs in response to these. It may even be valuable to think of them as a kind of conflict between you and us!

Collectively, considering these propositions shifts us from a teaching mode to a learning mode about our differing viewpoints. Rather than our being the person who alone knows what's right (has super vision) and seeks to teach that view effectively to our colleague or employee, we both become learners about ourselves and students of each other—specifically around our differences. If we productively doubt ourselves, we become learners about our own perspective as well as our colleague's or employee's perspective. Hearing how what we're saying makes sense and doesn't (where the gaps are, or what the other is confused about) allows us to test our own thinking, be clearer about what we mean—not to better ensure that the other gets it but rather to decide whether we think we should even change our mind about what we think.

This makes us vulnerable to finding limits to our viewpoint. Our not making sense may be a consequence of the other person's inability or unwillingness to listen, or it may be because there are gaps in our logic. We may be missing vital information or important contextual background, or we may be making unshared assumptions about the importance of certain information. Our meanings may be the source of the misunderstanding.

We also want to learn how the other sees the situation from her own perspective. This offers us the possibility of seeing things differently. To begin with, her perspective may help us better define our own. Moreover, we may learn that hers is another important,

Notepad 4.

Deconstructive Propositions	Your Reactions
1. There is probable merit to my perspective.	
2. My perspective may not be accurate.	
3. There is some coherence, if not merit, to the other person's perspective.	
4. There may be more than one legitimate interpretation.	
5. The other person's view of my viewpoint is important information to my assessing whether I am right or identifying what merit there is to my view.	
6. Our conflict may be the result of the separate commitments each of us holds, including commitments we are not always aware we hold.	
7. Both of us have something to learn from the conversation.	
8. We need to have two-way conversation to learn from each other.	
9. If contradictions can be a source of our learning, then we can come to engage not only internal contradictions as a source of learning but interpersonal contradictions (i.e., "conflict") as well.	
10. The goal of our conversation is for each of us to learn more about ourselves and the other as meaning makers.	

valid perspective we didn't consider because we were operating out of our own view. We also want to understand her perspective because we may learn that as much sense as we make to her, or our collaboratively contracted meanings make, her own initial meaning may make it difficult to switch. This learning process assumes that for some people to change they need to be able to understand their own view and its limits.

When we introduced you to the deconstructive propositions, we urged you (as usual) to keep track of your reactions to them. We'd like you to turn to those now. Although the propositions may help you challenge the conflict assumptions of which you are already aware, your reactions to the propositions can be mined for the purpose of identifying further assumptions. For example, we may have a big "no way" reaction to the deconstructive proposition that the goal of our conversation is to make sense of our conflict and not to convince the other of anything. We may feel "What's the point, then?"

If we can uncover what assumption generated this reaction, we may recognize that we are assuming that to be effective as leaders or managers means we ought to know correct answers. We might be assuming that not knowing means we are weak, or ineffective, or conversely that never or rarely doubting ourselves is a strength.

This may well connect up with another assumption, having to do with hierarchy and the notion that managers should know better and more than an employee, and this is why they are paid more and have greater decision-making powers and responsibility. In a feedback situation, we may be limited by our assumption that because we ought to know, our job is to tell the other, as opposed to seeing the other as a genuine collaborator in meaning making.

Alternatively, our reactions may seem as if they have less to do with assumptions we hold about conflict and difference in general, and more to do with assumptions we hold about the particular person with whom we are in conflict. We asked you to consider the ten propositions for deconstructing in the light of a real conflict situation you experience or have experienced. When you come to number eight ("We need to have a two-way conversation to learn from each other"), your primary reaction may be something on the order of "There's no way to have a two-way conversation for learning with this person; he doesn't listen in any way other than tactically. And everything he says has some ulterior motive."

Fine. Reactions of this kind direct us to important assumptions we hold about the particular person with whom we work. We are not saying the assumptions are false. We are saying that they are potentially changeable in at least two important ways. First, we don't know if the conversation might go unexpectedly with the person if another language for differences exists. Second, we don't know if the belief about the person is at all times valid. Has it ever really been tested? Have we tendentiously selected all past data that confirm the negative view of the person, and screened out all disconfirming data? Have we ever really explored our assumption about the person from an I-could-be-wrong position?

Once we use our reactions to make our assumptions explicit about conflictual language (whether of the general or the person-oriented sort), we can choose to pursue those that strike us as juiciest, that is, ripe for learning about our own meaning system. In this way, we can develop a highly personal and relevant internal learning curriculum about conflict.

There are a variety of ways to practice and nourish the language of deconstructive conflict (we take you further into the life of sustaining this language, and all the languages, in the next two chapters), but perhaps it suffices to conclude here by pointing out the three most common ways the intention, stance, and outcome of this language can be misunderstood.

Three Common Misunderstandings About the Deconstructive Approach

First, a language of deconstructive criticism is not a language of discounting one's own negative evaluation. It is not about assuming one is wrong and defusing one's own objections by internalizing a newly self-critical position that one is a walking distorter of reality. In the very first chapter of this book, while talking about the ever-present language of complaint, we made clear that we feel it is a risky and self-disrespecting move to ignore our own internal instruments just because they tell us there is something going on we do not like. We suggested that the road to happiness is not found through denying our own concerns or unfavorable evaluations and putting on a happy face.

Rather, the language of deconstructive criticism is about holding two simultaneous realities together: I respect myself to the extent of taking seriously that I have formed a negative evaluation, *and* I respect the other as an independent constructor of reality who might have quite a different picture of what is happening, a picture based on premises and assumptions that might usefully inform my own. How do I create a form of engagement that overinvests in (prematurely makes true) neither my construction of reality nor the other's? Whatever particular form the answer to this question takes (we give you examples in Chapter Nine), it reflects some kind of ongoing shared inquiry between the parties, a transformation of conflict from a clash of personalities into a contradiction for learning.

Second, practicing a language for deconstructive conflict does not leave one in paralysis of analysis, unable to act, merely better understanding the conflict (as if that by itself were an ultimate virtue). Whatever form the language takes, it includes two kinds of action: exploring and testing by both parties of the key assumptions that underlie their conflicting positions; and, if the conflict persists, a temporary or ultimate decision about how to carry on, rooted in the shared learnings that the language has so far created.

Third, a language for deconstructive conflict is not practiced first of all for the purpose of making the conflict disappear, or even reducing its intensity. It's even possible that such a language can be working well, but what it leads to is *more* conflict. Though the ultimate purpose of the language is valuable change and better functioning of the relationship or organization, it must be remembered that we exercise all the languages for the purpose of making our work settings richer contexts for learning. The kinds of change we are looking for are transformational. They go to the roots. They are not about fixes at the surface.

To fix over and over again new versions of conflict that may all derive from the same distorted way of constructing reality is not just costly for organizational life; it is a stand against the organization's learning from the lessons its dysfunctionality is trying to teach. As we have said, we learn these lessons—make the conflictual text of work life into a curriculum—by finding a way not to solve the curricular problems too quickly but to let the problems solve us.

The language of deconstructive conflict grows out of the belief that it is not conflict itself that is dangerous or dysfunctional; it is instead the familiar framing of conflict into the language of personal attribution and depreciative characterizing. This seventh and last language creates a context for transforming conflict into a respectable and learning-rich clash of contradictory premises, beliefs, and assumptions. The conflict persists. Its intensity may not lessen. Its engagement may even lead to additional conflict. But so long as the conflict is now framed in a fashion that promotes learning, all these circumstances name the growth of an organization's assets rather than its liabilities.

Part Three

Carrying on the Work

Chapter Eight

Running the Internal Languages

How can we sustain a relationship to our inner contradictions and Big Assumptions so that they can become ongoing resources for our learning rather than conditions of our mental captivity? What kinds of learning and changed behaviors may result if we do? The activities of the first four chapters in this book constitute a new kind of learning technology, built to facilitate people's personal learning. Use of the four languages illuminates our own dynamic equilibrium, the forces that keep it in place, and the possible means to transcend the power of this third force, our immunity to change.

The mental machine these languages build allows us to make important aspects of our mental life *the focus of* our attention (object in our knowing) rather than *the means of* our attending (subject in our knowing). We are temporarily able to make our inner contradictions and Big Assumptions what we look at rather than what we see through. This movement from subject to object "complexifies" our minds and is at the heart of our long-held view of the inner architecture of mental development and transformational learning. (For those of you who may be interested in a more formal treatment of this idea about the movement of subject to object, and how we have pursued it as researchers and theoreticians over the past twenty years, we have included several references to our work at the conclusion of this chapter.)

As useful as the technology of the first four chapters may be in temporarily making our inner contradictions and Big Assumptions visible, they can quickly fade from view. We reabsorb them. They take over once again—unless we use sustained action to prevent it.

We know of no successful McDonald's approach to substantive personal learning at work or anywhere else. No drive-through weekend or summer institute can by itself change our minds for the long run.

In our view, any worthwhile effort to enhance personal learning enables people to keep their inner contradictions and Big Assumptions in front of them, as objects of attention. Without this condition, people's working knowledge of their inner contradictions and assumptions easily slips and they resubject themselves to their former mental captivity. One of the best ways we can sustain and deepen a productive relationship with our inner workings is through fashioning new "conversational pockets," or "language communities" (sometimes as small as two people), which regularly make use of the languages discussed in this book.

In this chapter, we tell you a number of stories of the kinds of learning and behavioral change that can come out of these novel language communities, and the deliberate ways of working within them we have developed to use our Big Assumptions to disturb the equilibrium of our inner contradictions. In some cases, the stories arise out of personal learning groups one or both of us have facilitated over the years. These groups may be formed in the context of a semester-long course, meeting weekly for two or three hours each week; or in the context of an organization that has asked us to bring them a professional development opportunity by meeting monthly with a group of employees who may or may not have regular contact with each other at work. The organizations in which we have facilitated such groups are public and private, for-profit and nonprofit.

In some instances, members of the groups we initially facilitated go on to facilitate new groups without us, with other members of their organization (an outcome we encourage as people become more confident that they can fly solo). In some instances, we have maintained a consultative relationship with a group over the course of many years, dropping in regularly or irregularly as it serves the interest of the group.

Obviously, most of our stories arise out of these groups in which we have been privileged to participate, because we were there to listen and see what happened. However, the truth is that most of the ongoing learning and change that results from people making use of these languages goes on out of our sight. Some among the now thousands of people whom we have introduced to the languages—commonly in courses, workshops, consultations, or conference settings—go on to use them in some fashion in their work lives or personal lives. Occasionally, we hear from these people about their learning, and when the opportunity arises, we sit down with them, with a tape recorder, and capture their stories too. Some of these are included here as well.

At the end of Chapter Four, we briefly indicated a variety of ways we encourage people to thicken their relationship with their inner contradictions and Big Assumptions:

- *Observing the assumption in action:* What do I notice happens and does not happen as a result of holding my assumption as true? In what domains of my working—or living—do I notice my assumption being influential? Observing assumptions in daily experiences allows us to become fully acquainted with them. People often see facets of the assumptions, and circumstances in which they operate. We actively encourage people not to change their behavior, especially when they observe their assumptions at play, since in the beginning we are trying to increase the number of contact points we have with our assumptions, not make them disappear.

- *Staying on the lookout for natural counters and challenges to the assumption:* What spontaneous experiences do I notice that could suggest to me that my assumption might be inaccurate, not always applicable, or even wrong? Here we encourage people to regard their assumption as an hypothesis rather than the truth; we ask them to stay alert to any experiences or situations that seem to disconfirm the assumption. This activity is often a difficult one, as it requires us to become aware of and tuned into precisely the sort of occurrence that we have never been aware of before. Sometimes it helps to have people think in advance about what kinds of data or information constitute a challenge to the truthfulness of their assumption before they begin their lookout.

- *Writing the "biography" of the Big Assumption:* How long have I lived with this assumption? When was it born, and under what circumstances? What has helped it grow up? Have there been any significant turning points in its development? What is its life expectancy? Our intention here is to dig up the roots of the assumption, and in doing so make its history an object of attention. We come to learn that our Big Assumption is not us; rather, it is something we have lived with very closely.

• *Designing a safe, modest test of the assumption*: What can I risk doing, or resist doing, that might seem inadvisable if I held my Big Assumption as true, in order to learn what the results would actually be? We hold three criteria for a good test. First, it has face validity and can yield data that seem likely to be relevant to testing the assumption (including data that would call one's assumption into doubt). Second, there are no large-scale risks, even if the assumption turns out to be applicable. Third, it is actionable in the near-term, that is, relatively easy to carry out within a reasonable window of time.

• *Examining the results of the experimental test:* What did I learn from this test? Was it a fair test—did I really give myself a chance to learn whether the Big Assumption is in some way a distortion? What are the implications of this test for my relationship with the Big Assumption? What next test would I like to design and carry out? The intent of this activity is to encourage the learner to engage in an iterative process of seeing-doing-reflecting, which is likely to increase the depth of learning. We have been surprised by the many unanticipated, powerful results of people's experiments; frequently their tests lead to seeing issues and assumptions of which they were totally unaware.

Each of these activities helps to keep important aspects of our meaning-making object rather than subject, helps us to have our assumptions (for review, reconsideration, and possible reconstruction) rather than our assumptions having us (we are not aware of them or responsible for them; they run us). In some cases, people move through these activities neatly and sequentially; more often, they serve as rough guides for staying on track, begin to blend into each other, take place simultaneously, and are entered and reentered as the individual or the group sees fit. In the stories that follow, you see how one or another, or some combination, of these guiding activities seemed especially useful as an anchor or pivot in a person's learning process.

Susan's Story

Susan participated in a semester-long graduate seminar for educators on reflective practice and transformational learning that met three hours a week. As part of the seminar, all participants kept a journal of their own personal learning, prepared a packet of materials to give class members for consultation purposes, and wrote a final paper about their learning in the course. Susan's story is drawn from these documents (with her permission, of course; all the stories in this chapter appear with the permission of the principals).

Early in the semester, Susan identified a first-draft version of a Big Assumption. She saw it was keeping her in a state of ineffectiveness regarding her commitment to being a teacher and learner open to diverse ideas. It came in three parts:

> I assume (1) that I actually should be judging everything and everybody, and (2) that my judgments, which I can document so well (thus convincing at least myself), are invariably correct. Furthermore, (3) those whom I've judged to be inadequate should be taken to task by the appropriate authorities.

Observing the Assumption in Action

Susan viewed her Big Assumption as a juicy one (that is, there was a lot of energy and interest in it, one of our criteria for a decision to pursue developing a deeper relationship with the assumption) and was ready for the next step: observing the assumption in action. It turned out—perhaps a twist of fate—that the seminar class itself was one of the richest venues for Susan to observe her assumption in action. Right off the bat, she was critical about a fellow student.

In her journal, Susan tracks her observations over several weeks, beginning with her first awareness of being judgmental:

> I was already aware that I was intimidated by this classmate, Jo, who had taught at a renowned university, was a staff developer there, and was also a corporate trainer. I remember reacting to her telling us all this during introductions on day one and thinking *It's Dr. Jo, Dr. High-Powered*. Then I noticed that not only did she tend to be the first to speak in answer to the seminar professor's invitations, but that she tended to speak directly to him rather than include the rest of us. I sensed that we weren't the ones who counted.

Susan observes another instance of her Big Assumption operating:

> I was galled by what I saw as her sense of herself vis-à-vis the pro-
> fessor. Not only was he the only one who counted, but she was his
> peer! She gave him feedback on how he handled the class.

Susan sees that over time her judgments about Jo become
harsher. She describes the next occasion she sees her Big Assumption in gear:

> Jo always had the right answer, which I saw as invariably a simple
> one. At the rare time when she wasn't rehashing the obvious, Jo's
> comments were so characterized by alliterative acronyms, other
> jargon, and/or bizarre phraseology as to be incomprehensible to
> me. . . . She seemed unable to think clearly.

When it was Jo's turn to be consulted by the class, Susan found
new opportunities to observe her assumptions in action. From the
start of the session, Susan was critical of Jo, saying:

> Despite her calling it a preparation packet, it didn't consist of
> the necessary attributes of a preparation packet. The narrative
> consisted of a meager three double-spaced pages, followed by forty-
> five (!) unexpurgated, often single-spaced, pages of student jour-
> nals with no explanation of how to use them to understand the
> case, and two articles rather than the one requested, relating to
> the material. Her description of the case was not only brief, but so
> inadequate that I didn't feel I understood what was going on well
> enough to comment on it.

To Susan the session was one big problem, with ever-mounting
evidence that no one understood Jo's convening case, including (to
Susan's mind) the professor. Toward the end of the convening, a
new problem emerges when a student, Andy, voices anger "about
being given such an incomplete, incoherent packet," while another
student, Rita, counters this saying, "Just because it doesn't look like
a lot of time and thought went into it, it doesn't mean there wasn't."
Susan feels Rita is "coming to Jo's defense." She voices her agreement with Andy's viewpoint. Susan sums the session up like this:

In what had become a pattern that I didn't like, I saw the validity of Andy's and my criticisms of Jo's packet being blunted by Rita's statement that "the packet worked for me." Grrrr! How could it possibly have "worked" for anyone? There was no *there* there. Is Rita different from me? Could she really find a *there* there?

Now, in our view, Susan is doing a great job here with the first step of paying attention to how her assumption is operating. Recall that the purpose of this first step is not to try to change one's thinking or behavior at all. In fact, we strongly advise against overly quick changes since such a stance is likely to get us into the familiar routine to better ourselves, thus eliminating the possibility to transform ourselves. Susan now had plenty of material to see her assumption in action (she later reflects how her Big Assumption "had her," saying, "Oh, how crazy I was being driven!"), and she was able to honor the imposed limit that she not try to change anything during the period of her self-observation.

Staying on the Lookout for Natural Counters and Challenges to the Assumption

To keep the momentum of gaining distance from their Big Assumptions, Susan and her classmates were invited to stay on the lookout for natural counters and challenges to their assumptions. This step continues the theme of not trying to change one's thoughts or behaviors too quickly, and adds the quest for any experiences or information that could cast doubt on the truthfulness of one's assumption. This can be a difficult step, and it is impossible to anticipate when we will see a counter or a challenge (even if everyone else looking on is certain that a counter or challenge is right in front of our nose!).

Susan found this a tough, if not impossible, assignment. In her characteristically witty, honest, and self-deprecating way, she says, "It's no doubt connected to my ability to convince myself so thoroughly that I'm right!" In Susan's own retelling of her critical, judgmental reactions to Jo's convening session, there is indeed good reason to suspect that there were data to cast doubt on her assumption that her judgments are invariably correct. Most notable is the fact that Rita expressed assessments of Jo's material that were contrary to her own.

Susan did not construct this as useful information to her own learning, we suppose, because she was so certain that her assessment of Jo was correct. Hearing that Andy felt as she did was probably more evidence to Susan that she was right. Still, a slight crack in her certainty may have begun during this session, as she asks herself, "Is Rita different from me? Could she really find a *there* there?"

It may be easier for *us* to see how Rita's comment could have been a productive challenge to Susan, since we do not have the same investment in the situation as does Susan. That Susan had a bit of distance may help us understand how, in the very next session, she ends up being compelled to question one of her assumptions. During the next class, a classmate talks about a very problematic student he has had in his own teaching: "He's extreme . . . but ideally you can benefit from somebody off the grain. Everybody knows 'Here he goes again' once he opens his mouth . . . but you can learn something from that." Another student then talks about how the problem person himself may not get the full learning experience available from being in the class, but he probably gets more good than he would if he were not in the class.

No one could predict that these ideas would be seen by Susan as challenges to her own thinking, yet she experiences a powerful challenge to her assumption that people she is critical of ought to be taken to task. Susan recalls her reactions to these ideas:

> Light bulb in my head and heart. To think of the problem person "as if" they were sent to me to learn from. While I can't articulate why, ever after I felt differently about Jo. All that had driven me crazy became benign. Jo seemed more like a puppy trying, but unable, to do right than a malevolent hurricane trying to drown my parade. I no longer assumed that Jo was the problem, instead recognizing that *I* had a problem with *her*.

Designing a Safe, Modest Test of the Assumption

Earlier we said that the steps for keeping distance from our assumptions could blend with each other and take place simultaneously. Susan's process reflects one of those instances where the very moment of experiencing a challenge turns into a test of one's assumption. Even though people typically set out with an intentional test design (one that meets the various criteria for a good test), it is possible, as with Susan, to find oneself in a naturally occurring test. In Susan's case, this was a kind of mind experiment. Such a test involves trying on a new frame or mental model to interpret old material.

When a fellow student talks about always being able to "benefit from someone off the grain," Susan takes this to her experience with Jo and experiments with the idea that she can learn something from her. In doing so, she lets go, however temporarily, of the frame she has historically held, sustained by her Big Assumption that problem people ought to be taken to task. By considering a different way of making sense of her experience with Jo, Susan begins to make it explorable. Instead of being so "Big" (meaning, taken as true), it becomes just what it is: an assumption (that is, it *may* be true).

Examining the Results of the Experimental Test

One unexpected test result is that Susan realizes a new Big Assumption she holds, one that she feels underlies the others:

> I think at the heart of those assumptions there is a competition, a kind of assumption that someone else's gain is my loss, that I need to prove myself at someone else's expense to be "valued," or respected, or to get what I need.

Susan sees how Jo's accomplished CV got her believing that she has to prove herself, or that her chances of being valued are at risk. Her criticisms of Jo, she begins to consider, may be fueled by a need to reduce the size of the competition.

The main results from Susan's examination: there is a mix of constancy and change in her Big Assumptions. What has changed is her assumption that those whom she judges to be inadequate must be taken to task by appropriate authorities; she says "It is no longer important that a Just God punish the iniquitous" in her sight. Still, perhaps unchallenged and unchanged as yet is her first Big Assumption that she should judge everyone (now Jo is like a little puppy trying to do right, and by implication she is not succeeding), as well as her second Big Assumption that her judgments are correct. Susan's words capture this mix:

> Suddenly, it was OK with me that Jo was who she was. How much did her presence really mess up the class? Some off-the-wall comments that everyone largely ignored, and one ill-conceived consultation. Mess up the class, nothing! Throughout the semester, she continued to behave as bizarrely as ever. Acronyms, quick answers, and malapropisms abounded. As far as I was concerned, so what? So what if Jo wasn't punished?

Another result from Susan's test can be seen by following a cluster of Big Assumptions from which we can infer Susan was operating initially: she assumes that it is a problem that Jo is "incompetent and bizarre." Closely related is an assumption that Jo is the problem. A third assumption: *I can't learn from a problem student.* It follows from the assumptions that Susan initially believes that Jo must therefore change for things to improve. One of Susan's explicit assumptions, "those whom I judge to be inadequate should be taken to task by the appropriate authorities," identifies Susan's belief about how that change ought to occur.

But after Susan's "a-ha" following her classmates' comments, this whole cluster of unnamed assumptions seems to change:

> It does not have to be a problem that Jo is incompetent and bizarre (because I see now that I can learn from her, even as a problem student). I therefore assume that *I* am the source of making this into a problem (by not having seen how she could be a resource to my learning), and therefore I can change this into not being a problem (I can learn from someone like her).

Taking Stock

Susan's shifting assumptions now open her to learn from "problem student" Jo. To us, this is an extraordinary shift. What was impossible has become possible. Closed becomes open. In being open, Susan learns from Jo—though she does not exactly name this yet—that the ball is in her court as to how to react to people whom she regards as incompetent. This is especially critical for Susan in light of her self-crafted professional goal to be more tolerant of her students' diverse perspectives and her personal goal to get along better with people.

By making more distinct what she melded before—incompetence automatically led to a problem, and a problem automatically led to accompanying negative affect—Susan now sees that incompetence is not automatically equated with a problem. If there is not a problem, there need be no hard feelings.

Susan has begun to develop her ability to regard people whom she sees as incompetent in a neutral, tolerant, even caring way. Even if she is in a supervisory relation with such persons and has some responsibility for their performance, even if she is without a doubt correct in her evaluation of them, this developing capacity increases the chances she can be of greater help to them. It is important to note that had Susan somehow let go completely of her critical stance toward Jo, she would have lost the opportunity to transform the relationship between the cognitive contribution to her problem with Jo (her well-documented, well-reasoned criticisms) and her affective contribution (how she necessarily feels about what she knows is true about Jo).

Also, and very important, Susan has begun to get some distance from her core competitive assumption that her competitor must be publicly punished in order for her to get what she needs. (This idea, that her gain must come at the expense of someone else's loss, is now visible and explorable.) Jo can still be incompetent and not get punished; and Susan can still be valued (or be respected, or be accepted, or belong). Susan's inner world, and her outer world as a result, are undergoing a significant change.

We are not suggesting, nor would Susan, that this is a story (borrowing on her religious metaphors) of entering some Promised Land. There are inevitably further discoveries concerning her Big Assumptions that await Susan's ongoing journey, as there are for all of us. Susan may be completely right in her harsh judgment of Jo, but her own admirably honest account of the "special interests" she brings to formulating her criticism should at least make us somewhat suspicious. Nowhere in her account has she yet created a challenging relationship to her certainty of correctness in her evaluation.

But we do not intend these stories to represent some accomplishment of all the learning we may sense is possible in the processes the stories reflect. We intend them instead as testimonies to people's creativity and courage to make use of the languages on behalf of processes that are rarer than we may realize—the processes of changing how we make meaning, the very shape of our thinking and feeling. It is one thing to create an original idea out of our existing state of mind; it is another actually to alter our state of mind itself.

Postscript

Susan tested—in a completely different context—her assumed need to judge and see wrongdoing punished, in an effort to find out if she could apply her new learnings to anyone other than Jo. Could she sustain her new distance from a previously Big Assumption? Susan hoped to test how transformative her changes were:

> One critical attribute of transformative learning is that it's got some staying power. At midnight the dress doesn't return to rags, the coach to a pumpkin, and the coachmen to mice. That which has changed becomes a comfortable part of an expanded self. Was what I'd learned truly transformative, or was it merely a fleeting change in attitude?

Because she saw how her Big Assumption manufactured a kind of ineffectiveness regarding her commitment to being open to diverse ideas as both a teacher and a learner, Susan chose her own teaching of art as a context to answer this question.

> As a result of having accepted the gift of Jo, would I continue to be more tolerant, more able and willing to teach a class that was composed of anything other than "fifteen me's?" If [the class in which I had been a student] was a place where I got to discover and practice transformations in my interpersonal being, [in the class in which I am the teacher, which I call Awesome Arts], I have been able to continue practicing. With that practice my newly transformed self has become closer to feeling like my own self.
>
> My goals in leading Awesome Arts were twofold. I wanted to ameliorate the well-documented negative effects of our culture on

girls and wanted to teach them some art concepts. As usual, I felt the need to be giving them a lot and had planned all kinds of activities. In my over-achieving, over-kill, over-determined kind of way, I didn't want them to waste their time goofing around and having fun all day at camp!!

Confession: I hate first days of teaching. It's such a strain to do what I assume I need to, to get everyone to feel comfortable with each other and trust me. Previously, part of the difficulty I had with getting everyone to feel comfortable with each other was my own inability to feel comfortable with everyone. (Hey, all some of them wanted to do was goof around on their summer vacation, just to name one major offense against humanity!) Having had my tolerance transformation, however, I began to establish a model of tolerating them all myself.

Given that age range, the girls were light years apart in their level of physical and developmental maturity. Some were kids and some were "cool." I had no preference. Something inside me was different. I didn't insist that they get along with each other, but showed that I got along with everyone. As annoying as I found the less mature girls' babyishness, I let it go. By the end of the week, it had diminished. As intimidating as I found the more mature girls' cool aloofness, I approached them (somewhat coolly and aloofly). It turned out they, too, were just kids. I "did" almost nothing, just sat in that room and talked with whomever I happened to be sitting near, making sure that I sat near different people.

My inclination was to recoil from much of what they had to say about their hatred of their younger siblings, parents, and selves. Although everything inside me wanted to shut it up (and I had a rationale to do so: wasn't I supposed to be building self-esteem, not listening to Jean chant "I'm stupid"?), I could feel that shutting it up was futile and destructive. To shut that hate out of public language was to trap it in the psyche.

For reasons having to do with all kinds of things you don't want to hear about, the class took place in a clay studio with a number of potting wheels. I probably could throw on a wheel (having learned to do so twenty years ago), but it's not something I feel secure about doing or know how to teach. The girls wanted to use the wheels. I didn't freak out; I didn't say no; I didn't cover up my ignorance. I explained to them that I couldn't teach wheel throwing but would ask one of the pottery assistants to do so. He gave a very nice demonstration, told them that the thing to do was fool around with the wheels and that he'd be available if they had questions. Most of the girls "threw" everyday, which is to say they put lumps of clay on the wheel and pushed them around and produced short, stubby, wobbly things with holes in the middle. This wasn't my problem and as soon as it wasn't, it was clear that it wasn't a problem for them either; I saw that they saw those clunky chunks of clay quite differently than I did.

In order to balance my sense of responsibility that I teach something and their right to goof, I offered a "class" every morning which each girl would choose to take part in or not. What had changed was that I genuinely did not care. If they wanted to try an exercise in composition, fine; if not, fine. Sometimes they would doodle for over an hour, a "worthless" activity that usually makes me crawl the walls. Here they were, privy to my extensive expertise and they're wasting their time!! I noticed that Arielle had a good sense of design. Nonetheless, she spent mornings making tiny, poorly composed pencil drawings of that adolescent girls' old standby motif, horses. Arielle, the coolest, the punkiest rebel of all, was not about to do what the teacher told her.

This teacher had learned *not* to tell. On the third morning, as I passed her, I mentioned that I thought she might like to do some big paintings of horses. She sort of nodded. I let it go. Previously I would have given her the paper, paint, and brush. The next day she asked me why I thought she'd like to paint horses. I asked if one of the things she liked about horses was the movement (I figured it was, since she always drew them prancing or jumping). She agreed. I explained that pencil was a really hard way to show movement since it doesn't flow, whereas paint does. Similarly on an 8" × 12" piece of paper, the artist's arm can't flow, which mitigates against representing a moving creature. At that point, I helped her get all the materials she needed. White and black paint on charcoal gray 24" × 36" paper. I could see her surprise and pleasure at what she'd accomplished. She hung it on the wall.

When Jean asked me why Arielle wasn't cleaning up when everyone else was (which was really bothering me; I'd asked everyone to clean up several times), I (by this time, reflexively) said I didn't know and suggested that she ask Arielle herself. She did. Arielle said she was going to clean up as soon as she finished the piece she was working on. She rapidly finished and started cleaning up. Problem handled.

By the end of the week, everyone was talking with each other, they seemed to accept each others' foibles, there was less talk about hatred for their families and selves and more about love for their pets. The studio had us fill out an evaluation together—the negatives had to do with facilities; the positives with projects we'd done and the comfort of the group. Looking back, I see that my growth as a student permitted my growth as a teacher. Previously I had felt little tolerance for someone or some dynamic messing up my group. Now, over this week, through my increased tolerance, I had contributed to the development of a community of tolerance.

We can rarely anticipate if, when, and how a person will push her envelope. Susan's story depicts her efforts to become more of the person she wishes to be. Once she began to be disturbed by her Big Assumption, she began to disturb it. The results—new thinking and new behavior—were self-reinforcing and self-renewing.

Emily's Story

Emily's learning story begins when she participated in the four-column exercise while attending an institute. On her own initiative, she chose to pursue exploration of her Big Assumption, developing a small language community through periodically talking with one of us or another institute participant. The following is her story, told to us many months after her initial exposure to her Big Assumption.

Emily constructed the conceptual map shown in Figure 8.1 during the four-column exercise.

Figure 8.1. Emily's Four-Column Map.

Frontline Commitment	Responsibility	Hidden Commitment	Big Assumption
I am committed to the importance of . . . More focused time to do what I think is most important in my work.	*I do what people ask of me. I even anticipate people's needs and act accordingly.*	*I am also committed to the value of being seen by others, including myself, as a valued member of my department.*	*I assume that if I were to do less in my department I'd be less valued. I assume my value isn't inherently in me, but is tied to what I do.*

Observing the Assumption in Action

Leaving the institute with her Big Assumption in mind, Emily spends weeks observing herself while at work, keeping track of occasions when she is aware that these particular assumptions are in gear. One day she accidentally discovers that her same assumptions are at play in her home life. Although she is intellectually aware that it is possible, even likely, that her assumptions accompany her regardless of her whereabouts, she finds it powerful to see herself acting similarly with her family as with her colleagues. As is often the case, the situation that becomes such a powerful emblem of one's assumption in action is a tiny, incidental matter: Emily sees herself anticipating one of her children's needs for milk at the dinner table.

The consequence of her observations, both at work and at home, is that Emily sees that the "counter" behaviors she identified in her second column (self-responsibility) are far more frequent and prevalent than she was aware. Her awareness has deepened; she says, "I see how I make myself totally 'necessitated' for things to run," "I make myself indispensable in any situation." She sees how "any" situation includes what she views as "petty stuff," such as anticipating her thirteen-year-old child's need for a glass of milk and getting him one.

Staying on the Lookout for Natural
Counters and Challenges to the Assumption

Watching herself, she comes to realize that her need "to do, in order to be valued" is a broad, pervasive theme in her life. This realization seems to lead her to another realization, that "other people feel that they have value in and of themselves and not by what they do." Emily experiences her latest realization—that there are people who have value by being who they are rather than by what they do—as a challenge to her assumption. She feels motivated by this contrast between herself and others, saying, "I had to look at it. And so I started playing with it."

Designing a Safe, Modest Test of the Assumption

Emily begins her plans to behave a little differently "to see if this assumption still holds up as well." Here she enters the realm of explicitly testing her assumptions. At first, these are very small tests, just as we suggest. She decides to use her home front as the first testing ground, to see what happens if she acts differently in response to the small, "petty stuff."

She recounts how once when her child asked her to get him a glass of milk, "I said 'No, I'm not available this minute' and I just sat down." This was a tiny test of her assumption: someone was asking her to do something that she did not genuinely feel like doing at that moment; she responds differently than usual; she denies the request and tells her son why; and the earth does not give way beneath her feet.

This was the first of Emily's modest and safe tests of her Big Assumption. The idea of these tests is to design and run small, safe tests, where even if the worst suspicions are confirmed (in this case, if Emily finds out that people do not value her as a person, but only as a "doer") the price to pay is not too high. The goal of these tests is to generate data that can shed light on the Big Assumption. These tests often involve altering our usual behavior (actions or words) in ways we don't ordinarily permit ourselves, given that we hold our Big Assumptions as true.

Rarely is the outcome of these tests the discovery that our assumption is flat-out wrong; more often we come to question its global, undifferentiated quality. We discover the nature of the circumstance in which the assumption tends to be warranted, but we come to consider there may be many circumstances in which it does not. After all, we call our Big Assumptions "big" because they are taken as truths and thus function too broadly, serving as a screen for far too many specific situations and circumstances. Even in cases where one concludes that a Big Assumption is false, our goal for the person is to develop a new assumption that is variegated and contextualized; that is, "In situations of this kind, when I feel this particular way, when I am with this type of person, only then does my assumption that the world works in this way tend to be accurate."

Examining the Results of the Experimental Test

Emily recalls her new way of responding to her son during this period of her exploration, saying, "If he'd asked me for something and it was convenient for me, I would do it. But if it wasn't, I'd say 'no' and explain." The consequence: "We were fine." She continues:

It used to be that in my mind it was that if I know someone needed something, I would do it. But I gave myself permission to notice that, yes, they would like to have it done, but I did let myself feel I didn't necessarily have to do it. My kids accepted it. At first it was a little strange. It started out with little things, like the milk, that I wouldn't jump up and make happen, and then it got to be bigger things. The news for me was that I didn't feel as bad as I expected to feel!

Designing a Safe, Modest Test of the Assumption—Again

With a newfound sense of the possibility that her value does not have to depend on doing, Emily decides to up the ante in her exploration and make small changes to her behavior while at work. Again, her intent here is to test the accuracy and limits of her assumption, since it is quite plausible that although her assumption might not apply to home life, it still could apply to work. Her clarity about what more she wants to learn about her assumption leads to a next round of tests.

Progressive tests, like Emily's, are vehicles to deepen our understanding of when a Big Assumption tends to be warranted and when it does not. Results from such progressive tests help us reshape a Big Assumption to reflect these deeper understandings.

Emily recalls her first experiments conducted at work:

There's the whole layer of things I've always done that I thought were so important to other people. So the next sequence of things was to check some of that out, because it was complicating my life to try to accommodate some of these needs, and it seemed that it was so important somehow that I be in certain places or do certain things. So I'd indicate that I was willing to do it, whatever it was, but the person needed to let me know, in the spectrum of things, just how important it really was.

Emily gives us an example of a meeting scheduled for a certain hour that means she will be unable to keep a plan with her children. The new behavior is: "I'd simply check with my colleague running the meeting—did it make a real difference if I couldn't be there?"

Examining the Results of the New Experimental Test

Generalizing what she learned from these experiments, Emily says:

> I realized there was a whole category of things I was convincing
> myself were important and that when push came to shove, it wasn't
> important for the other person. And if they weren't willing to ac-
> knowledge that it had any importance to them, why should I be
> convinced it was so important? And I learned that sometimes it *did*
> make a difference to the person, but then it was easier for me. It
> narrowed the number of things I felt I had to do.

Designing a Safe, Modest Test of the Assumption—Yet Again

Up until now, we have been following Emily's intentional experiments. We have seen how specific behavioral changes led her to
find out that she does not have to "do, do, and more do." She can
set limits, some with people's input, and not feel badly for enact-
ing those limits. These new behaviors also seem to have led her to
begin thinking differently about her self-worth.

As in Susan's case, Emily next finds herself engaging in what
amounts to a mind experiment. Such experiments do not involve
anything in the outside world; indeed, no one would notice a mind
experiment in process. It is entirely internal. It is trying on a different way of thinking, including making comparisons and contrasts that one has not considered making before, and seeing what
happens internally as a consequence. These don't need to begin
intentionally, either; as in Emily's case, this different thinking
seems to just happen, and then one becomes aware of a new possibility or feeling. Emily describes what happened for her:

> I've been lucky enough over my life to have this host of friends. It's
> a small group, but they're these people who no matter when I get
> together with them, they feel close. It feels like we pick up where
> we left off. We talk about things that are important to us. They're
> very special relationships, which I know are intermittent, but feel
> permanent to me. I was realizing that I've been seeing that it's very
> existential how people feel. Like if I'm not doing what they cur-
> rently want or if I'm not somehow or another reminding them of
> how essential I am to them, then in my mind I pale in importance
> to them. I realize I haven't credited them with a constancy that I

know I feel. I know there are just some special people for me, and that it really isn't what they do or how often I see them. There's just a connection that's important to me and I'm grateful that I have them in my life. And I started being able to think that this is what my goal is, to be connected, in some bond with other people as opposed to the very busy do-it-all I've been.

Juxtaposing her relationship with special friends to their relationships with her, she appreciates that other people may have the same level of constancy in their feeling about her as she does for them, a constancy that does not depend on her continuously "doing for." This frees her up, along with the clarity of her newly developing realization that what she wants from her life is to be intrinsically, not instrumentally, connected to others. She has begun to separate out an experience of "constancy" that does not depend on creating in others an experience of her "indispensability."

Examining the Results of the Experimental Test—Yet Again

Emily sees that being indispensable became the mistaken means of accomplishing the clarified ends. She also sees that maybe the end of being connected can be obtained by other means. We see this as a critical juncture for her. Like Susan, she gets a kind of distance on a situation she was embedded in before, or subject to; new distinctions sustain that distance; new internal choices and outer behaviors ensue.

This shift enables her to let go of needing people to see her importance in what she *does*. She sees that those few people who do not appreciate her for who she is are not in a position to develop a genuine bond with her. She sees that her prior existence, with her constant motion following her agreements to do whatever anyone asked her to, actually kept her from being connected to those people, and kept reinforcing her Big Assumption that she had to keep doing for them. She sums up the change she feels this way:

> Earlier I didn't want to know that it wasn't critical for me to be at a meeting. Or that it wasn't important to my child if I were home an hour later than usual. Now I'm seeing 'not so important' and *not* being indispensable as a relief, as opposed to a no-validation.

These experiments all name ways that Emily succeeds in sticking her big toe over the edge of the world she created with her nest of assumptions. The world is turning out not to be flat after all, and Emily feels that she can continue to explore it without fear that she will drop off the edge. The energy and learning drawn from running these experiments emboldens her to run an even bigger one.

Designing a Bigger Test of the Assumption

One of Emily's main work involvements—for which she was receiving no recognition in her compensation—was directing a traineeship, with central responsibility for the learning of nearly one hundred trainees. This was alongside a full load of other responsibilities. "Working for free" might previously have served the goal of indispensability for Emily, as somehow it may have been a wonderful way to feel valued. But this shifted for Emily:

> I realized it wasn't worth continuing to do this this way. . . . I made clear that I didn't want to quit being director of the traineeship, but that it had to be acknowledged as being a contribution to the department and somehow be counted, and until that happened I wasn't willing to do it anymore.

Describing what happens following this unprecedented decision, Emily says:

> They continued to act as if I was still directing the program! Even though I wrote an official letter! I was still sent the evaluations for trainees; the problems came to me. I just passed them back on. This went on for a couple of months, and when a new division director came on board, he came up to me and said, "I've heard you're doing wonderful educational things in the division, so I'm assuming you'll stay on in that capacity now that I'm director"! And I said, "Well, actually I resigned three months ago. And no one seemed to notice. I'd be happy to talk to you about it when you've got the time, because if you're willing to recognize the effort I would be willing to come back." His response was, "What do you mean, 'recognition?' Others are on committees, why do you need recognition for this?" And I said, "Shepherding 93 trainees a year through our division and keeping an eye on them is a little more

than committee work, but if you can find someone else to do it for no recognition, more power to you."

This was a whole new Emily at work, one running contrary not only to how she knew herself but also to the pervasive work culture of her field. Emily's test clearly got a bit bigger than declining her son's request that she be his waitress and bring him a glass of milk. Like the Bartleby (the Scrivener) of her own profession, she was asked to resume a taken-for-granted responsibility and said simply (and revolutionarily), "I prefer not to." In the process she risked losing both a job she valued and a precious sense of being valued by others at work.

Examining the Results of the Experimental Test

Although an expanding scope of assumption testing soon transcends our criterion of modesty, each brave explorer has to make decisions about how far beyond safe she is willing to go. To Emily, however, the momentum of her deepening self-respect has by this time become paramount. She feels she can live with the worst-case outcomes, should it turn out that way. The concrete outcome of her experiment is this:

> He later came back to me and offered to recognize my role directing the program as a proper percentage of my work. We had a couple of conversations about what I was doing and the time I was putting in, and he agreed to pay me for more than I had even asked to begin with!

And the price for her in carrying out this test?

> The sky didn't fall. I didn't get fired, and people aren't terribly angry at me that I'm aware of. Most important, I don't feel quite so much the victim in my life that I did. I feel like I'm a different person than I was last year when I started to think about all this stuff.

The Biography of the Assumption

For Emily, the biography of her Big Assumption came more clearly into view after she ran these revealing tests:

I grew up in an alcoholic family with pretty typical dysfunctional dynamics and limited choices of roles to play: (1) the Perpetrator, source of all disappointment, irresponsibility, and definitely the bad guy to be; (2) the Victim, the disappointed, disillusioned, and resentful character who, though seemingly blameless, has a generally painful part to play; and (3) the Rescuer, the character who, if he/she can't fix everything can at least make things better temporarily. Each interaction was a game of musical chairs with the object being to have your butt in the rescuer's seat at all costs! The game was played so fast that one never paused to consider what would happen if one stopped playing . . . but obviously the risk was being perceived as the dreaded Perp.

It's sad to believe that a powerful driving force even in my adult life could be reduced to such a simple old script, but it's true. Testing the Big Assumption for me entailed seeing what it felt like to be perceived as neither Victim nor Rescuer, and realizing that being viewed as the Perpetrator didn't necessarily mean much if I knew I wasn't in the game.

Taking Stock

By conducting and learning from a series of tests and explorations, Emily has transformed her original Big Assumptions ("I assume that if I were to do less in my department, I'd be less valued, and I assume my value isn't inherently tied to me but is tied to what I do"). In her case, she discovered that her Big Assumptions were not valid in any of the situations she explored. They went from being Big Assumptions (truths) to merely assumptions (possibly so) to rejectable (not so). Over the course of one year, she reconstructed her original assumptions about doing and being valued to this nest of assumptions:

- I assume that I matter as a person.

- I assume that I need to be the person who puts my needs into the mix, and that I should not count on others to do so.

- I assume that others are aware of their own level of need and that they will be honest with me about this when I ask them.

- I assume that there are/will be people who value me only for what I do, and I assume I can live with that. I am not so fragile that I will break.

- I assume that I can be both dispensable and valued. I assume I can say "no" and still be valued.

- I assume my personal relationships are developed and sustained primarily through shared experience of close feelings, and not primarily through my "doing."

Who could have known the course Emily's personal learning would follow, and the direction in which it would point her? Not us. Not Emily. Looking back to her first-column commitment, she said she needed more focused time to do what she thought was important. Time, her lack of it, seemed at first to be the issue. Even though having more focused time turns out to be a part of her new existence, that change is the consequence of deep inner changes she could not know she would make when she began.

The process of Emily's objectifying the Big Assumption that drives her inner contradiction leads her to see something that never occurred to her before: that she hasn't been entirely clear what is important to her. Without this realization, Emily might not have discovered that what she most longs for is to be more intrinsically connected to people. Without this clarity, one can imagine that even if she succeeds in having more time to do what is important to her, it is likely she will use it in a fashion that still leaves her dissatisfied. Her change process, like a complex, multilayer domino roadway, spread from an origin into unknown places and led to insights, questions, investigation, and understandings that she could never have anticipated at the beginning.

Peter's Story

Peter built his initial four-column map during an institute much like the one Emily attended. He and a few colleagues who attended the program together stayed in touch with each other around the work. Reflecting on where his journey of examining his Big Assumption—now several years along—has taken him, Peter says:

Thankfully, I'm at a point now where, having done all this thinking, talking with my "buddy" and other people, forcing myself to think about all this, using all the learning that has gone on—it has all helped to give me a perspective I'm firmly grounded in now, and I feel like I can actually stand on it, as opposed to being in quicksand where you just don't have any way of approaching something. You're wallowing and it's very difficult. Now it's ordered. I know how to approach the situation. The situation has order to it, there's a structure, I think, that has created a foundation I can stand on.

Peter's first construction of his inner contradiction is: "I am committed to the value and importance of being honest with myself and with the people I work with (column one); and I am committed to people liking me and thinking well of me (column three)." His first draft of his Big Assumption is: "I assume that if I do things that people do not like, then they will not like me, and [by implication] if they do not like me or think well of me it will be Intolerably Awful!" Peter's story traces the outlines of how he moved from this initial construction, to later recognizing that he was "wallowing" in the "quicksand" of powerful ways of thinking over which he had no control, to eventually having a new foundation on which to stand.

Observing the Assumption in Action

At the beginning of his process of leveraging his Big Assumption, Peter follows our suggestion not to try to alter his thinking or his behavior, but simply to observe. He watches himself carefully to see what he does in situations where he wants the other person to like him. What he sees over and over is that he expends enormous energy trying to find the right words to say, so that the other person will think highly of him. More often than not, the search for the right thing to say leads him to say things he does not necessarily believe.

Generalizing his discovery from watching himself, he says:

> What I found is that it was all the little things. It wasn't on issues of great importance. But I didn't realize all the times when I was compromising. You try to figure out 'What don't I like about what I'm doing? Why is it that I come to work and I feel this angst about just showing up?' And that's it. Those little compromises.

He recounts a situation when a student came to ask him for permission to reschedule an exam. Peter thought this was an unreasonable request, especially as it did not follow the school's policy, which clearly stated that exams could be rescheduled only under emergency situations. This was not an emergency situation. Nonetheless, Peter OK'd the student's request. He says, "It was easier for me to compromise being honest because I did it so I could say to the person what I thought they wanted to hear from me."

Through self-observation, Peter sees that his Big Assumption influences his behavior in worlds beyond his work as well. He says:

> I realized that the honesty issue is much more deep-seated in my personal nature, but I hadn't been willing to look at it. It was difficult to realize that it applied to my home relationships, really with everyone. It was easier to admit that I could be dishonest at work, because those people aren't as important to me as my family.

Staying on the Lookout for Natural Counters and Challenges to the Assumption

As with Susan and Emily, the steps for detaching from our Big Assumption often blur. Peter's journey shows how the first step of observing ourselves can also shed light on what we can learn from another step: seeking counterexamples. Peter has not been on the lookout for natural counters or challenges to his Big Assumption, but while watching for how his Big Assumption operates in his daily life, he spontaneously notices a number of "counter instances." He sees situations where he takes stands or actions he knows will lead to the other person's unhappiness with him, but he is nonetheless untroubled and undeterred.

He recounts an example:

> I was involved in an interview process in which I learned that one of the key members of the board had basically railroaded an interview. This fellow unilaterally engineered it so that two people from the search committee would be out the day I interviewed. I was outraged. I knew he would be outraged if I were to say anything, but I had to. After they made their decision, I in fact said something to the board. In the end, this man had to resign. I'm sure he was unhappy with me, but how he felt about me didn't matter. This was a big issue I wasn't about to compromise myself on.

As Peter makes sense of these apparent counterexamples, he recognizes that they are not counterexamples at all. He sees instead that they are situations that help him clarify further the conditions under which his Big Assumption becomes activated. In all the supposed counterexamples, Peter realizes that he doesn't care whether the person likes him or not. He realizes that he does not need everyone with whom he deals to like him or think well of him.

Looking over the situations when his Big Assumption operates, he is able to generalize that the key condition for engaging it is when he cares about the other's opinion of him. He redrafts his Big Assumption. The people whose opinions he cares about are people for whom he has a great deal of respect, or people he has to deal with on so regular a basis that their not liking him is something he would have to regularly experience, or people who have sufficient power or influence that they could act out of their dislike in ways that could harm or diminish him in some way.

Writing the Biography of the Big Assumption

When invited to consider the genesis of his Big Assumption, Peter recognizes its origin in his family. Recall that the intention of this step is to dig up the roots of the assumption, and in so doing make its history an object of attention. Very often, as in Peter's case, the biography is rooted in our childhood, a time when we are subject to a host of conditions and realities that do not have to exist in our adulthood. This step gives us the space in which to consider the validity of our Big Assumption in the current contexts of our adult lives.

Peter says:

> I realize that no one ever specifically said this to me, but it was one of those truths that seeped into me. As a young child, I was aware that my parents were both very well liked. People always received them very well. Like my dad; he's an easygoing, outgoing, bright man who everyone adored. Even my grandparents. I remember when I was at my grandmother's funeral—and there were so many people present. People I hadn't seen in years, even my 3rd grade teacher, and people I'd never met. But it definitely made a deep impression on me—my grandmother was liked by all these people. It must be really important in life to be liked. This was my perspective.

I never thought about this before. Deep down I know that I
must have believed that being liked was how I would be a valuable
member of my family. Clearly I couldn't have known back then
that all those people could have "liked" my parents and my grand-
parents out of respect for them and who they were. I see now how
being respected is a sustainable form of being liked; but they are
different. I couldn't have known that as a child.

Designing a Safe, Modest Test of the Assumption

Looking back, Peter recalls having run a large number of small
tests of his assumption. Using what he learned from his earlier self-
observations, Peter knew he had to run tests that involved people
whose opinion of him mattered. He also knew that his tests should
involve responding to small matters, and that his effort would be
to communicate his perspective honestly to the other person.

He recalls a test:

It was really a simple matter. Someone came to my office and asked
me for a personal day off the next day. I knew that wasn't going to
work, because one of his colleagues had just called in sick and was
fairly certain that she wouldn't be back for at least two days. So I
said to this fellow "I'm sorry, but that's not going to work tomorrow.
We're going to be short-handed already. We'll have to find a different way to handle what you need."

Examining the Results of the Experimental Test

Peter views the outcome of his experiment favorably: he is honest
in response to the person's request (he knows it isn't a good idea
to give the person the day off), and the person "didn't bite off my
head"; "as a matter of fact, he accepted my decision without bat-
ting an eye. I didn't feel like my decision was going to affect how
he felt about me. That was liberating."

Designing a Safe, Modest Test of the Assumption—Again

Another test Peter runs involves his "open door" policy. As the
chair of his department, Peter chooses to make himself available
to students and faculty through an open-door policy, which means

that people should feel free to come and talk whenever they wish. This is not an official policy, but rather more how Peter acts when people knock on his door. He feels strongly about never saying to people that he is too busy to talk with them when they need to talk, as he believes that this is "standoffish, and they'd think I think I'm more important than they are."

Peter recognizes that one way he is being dishonest with himself, and then with others, is by making himself available when he isn't, by setting aside his need to accomplish certain tasks when others ask him for his time. Intellectually, he knows that saying yes to people when they ask for time is a way to make himself more likeable. He realizes that this is at his expense. He also begins to rethink whether his less-than-full availability is even fair to people, as he can't fully listen while he is worrying about getting back to his other work.

So he experiments. He begins to leave his door open when he is available to talk with others, that is, times when he feels he can be interrupted at his work. When he feels pressure to attend to his work, he closes the door. Should someone knock while the door is closed, he decides he will let them know that he is not available at that moment but suggest a better time to talk.

Examining the Results of the Experimental Test—Again

Peter describes what happens with his new "open, open door" policy:

> I never would have anticipated it would go quite like this, but I feel like this simple little change has made a very big difference in the way that people talk to me and I talk to them. They actually like it better this way. Ironically, I think people respect me more for making the time for them, rather than my trying to squeeze them in.

Designing a Safe, Modest Test of the Assumption—Yet Again

Peter later runs a test with a typical situation that in the past has engaged his Big Assumption when a student requests special treatment.

> In this particular situation, the student came in and asked if he could miss Friday's clinic so that he could attend his best friend's wedding on Saturday. In my head, I was thinking "Well maybe,

maybe not." It depends on whether his reasons are strong enough to stand the test of time—how would this work if everyone came in and asked for what he did? As I listened, it became clear that the reason this student wanted to miss Friday was so that he didn't have to drive in Friday night's traffic. I couldn't accept that. And I told him that unfortunately I couldn't grant him his request. We talked, and I let him know that I understood how his plan would be easier for missing Friday, but I also let him know what his taking the day off under those circumstances would mean for the clinic, with our being one person short, and for his fellow students.

Examining the Results of the Experimental Test—Yet Again

Peter sees the results of this test as confirmation of his growing understanding that it is possible to meet his need to be honest with himself and others *and* his need to be liked, as he discovers himself in deeper communication with people.

> The difficult part is that you have to learn how to communicate your honesty. There are people skills involved. But once I decided to be honest, I found myself, like with this student, in a different kind of a conversation that was more respectful between both of us. It opened up lines of communication that wouldn't have been there before—what is there to talk about if you've told the person exactly what they wanted to hear? I realize that I assumed that if I were to come right out and ever say no to someone's request, that there would be nothing else to say. I was wrong about that.

And Further Testing

Exploring what it means to say no and be more honest with his sons is the next step. Peter describes a time when his thirteen-year-old son asked him for permission to attend a rock concert. Peter knew that his son wanted to go badly, and was also aware of a part of him that did not want to disappoint his son. However, he was also aware that he did not think it was a good idea to go to this particular concert with the particular friends with whom he was planning to go. Peter says, "As hard as it was, I told him that his mother and I weren't giving him permission to attend this particular concert. I talked with him about the ways we did not see it as in his best interests, and about how it is our job as parents to make those judgment calls."

And Further Examination of the Results

The results of this test? "He definitely didn't like that he couldn't go. But he didn't not like me. I was honest with him about why and he appreciated that. I didn't just say no."

Peter goes on to describe what he draws from this kind of test:

> The more I tried to do something to please the other, the less I pleased myself. But if I stayed true to my principles or pleased myself, I wasn't pleasing them and they wouldn't like me. . . . The two seem to grow and feed on each other. Figuring that out, seeing the dichotomy and trying to determine which was more important, or more importantly trying to figure out how to connect the two, is where the changes have occurred and where the challenges have been.

What Peter has figured out is that he does not have to frame this as an either-or reality. He has figured out that when only one need can be met, it must be his need to be truthful to himself, since otherwise he doesn't like himself. He says, "If I'm not honest, then I don't like myself. It's very hard to live with lying or not being honest to principles that you hold near and dear." Although he has concluded that he needs to like himself more than he must have others like him, this isn't to suggest that the other is no longer in the picture.

Peter Steps Back

As Peter reflects on what has changed for him over the past years, he generalizes from his various experiments. One important lesson for him has been the relationship between self-honesty and honesty to others:

> It was the little things, and so it was easier to compromise being honest because I did it so the other person . . . so I would say to the other person what I thought they wanted to hear from me. Only that gets layered. The problem is you can't just peel away the layers because no matter what you do eventually it's that you weren't being honest. Not only to yourself, but the other person could say "You weren't being honest with me." And that was true.

Another critical lesson is about the effectiveness of his strategy to get people to like him:

> Being honest *doesn't* usually result in not being liked. Maybe for the short term but not the long term. And if they don't like you at all, then it must be a really big issue that you'll never agree on. But those are much clearer. I realize now that those issues are much easier for me to figure out. And those are the ones I'm not willing to compromise on anyway. Besides, I know now that compromising never made a difference anyhow. Either the people liked me or they didn't.

Another significant change is in Peter's definition of what it *means* for the other person to like him. Whereas Peter used to assume that people could not separate him as the decision maker from the decision he was making, he now sees that they are distinct. Asked how he would describe what his third-column commitment is now, regarding people liking him, he says:

> Being liked, as I meant it a couple of years ago when we started this, is gone. Maybe my commitment is still about being liked, but it's for a different reason. *Like* no longer becomes the correct word in the commitment. I want people to like me for the right reasons. I don't want them to like me just to like me. That has different levels. I want them to like me because they respect me for being true to who I am.

Perhaps most important to Peter is the change in his clarity and confidence about the critical importance of self-honesty and having a method for keeping himself honest.

> What's amazing to me is these are really very small, tiny little things, none of which I would consider direction-changing in my life, but they're behavior that wasn't true to what I believe. I think what I tended to do was to subvert what was important to me, that I would repress that and let these things just go on because dealing with what I was repressing was a much more difficult thing to do because I didn't have a way of dealing with it. I have clarified the value of being honest with myself. I've ordered the importance of it—it's the most important thing. Now I have an approach with an order to it, so there's a structure I can use. I think that's what has

served as building the foundation I can stand on. I always know exactly what I have to look for from the start, which is where do I really stand, and how might my wish to have the other person respect me lead me off track.

Taking Stock

Peter challenged his original assumption ("I assume that if I do things that people do not like, then they will not like me, and [by implication] if they do not like me or think well of me it will be Intolerably Awful!") through a series of tests over several years. He has reconstructed his original assumption to this nest of assumptions:

- I assume that pleasing oneself through being honest is not necessarily contrary to pleasing someone else.

- I assume that it's wrong to say or do what I think other people want me to just because they want me to.

- I assume that there are ways to communicate my position honestly without leading the other to not like me.

- I assume that people can distinguish between a decision and the decision maker; people can feel unhappy about a decision and not dislike the decision maker.

- I assume that people can like the fact that you are honest with them even though they dislike what you are saying.

- I assume that people can have different reactions to the same event over time (a person could be unhappy with me in the moment, and later feel fine).

When we first formally interviewed Peter, he was actually in the middle of a preoccupying, high-stakes, still-unresolved work complication that he was aware implicated just the issues to which he had been attending. A new boss had arrived on the scene with whom Peter shared a problematic past, and before long there were myriad opportunities to consider how honest he was willing to be.

I haven't sorted it out yet. I'm not sure. It may mean my job. What will I do if it comes to that? I think I know, but I'm not sure. But thinking about it has made it much clearer to me what I have to look at.

Thinking about it is another significant change for Peter. Using the new technology as a tool, Peter has learned how to systematically approach situations that previously he was merely "coping with," what today he would call "wallowing in quicksand." His confidence in himself and his ability to proactively notice and tackle situations has consequently increased. The combination of his deeper understanding about himself as well as using the four-column method contributes to Peter's feeling up to the task of tackling the big size of his situation:

> I came back to that Big Assumption and realized it was really going to be put to a very big test in this case. I feel comfortable having given all this thought to at least being able to work through it. While I'm worried about it, I wasn't scared that I wouldn't be able to approach it in some kind of reasonable manner and understand why I was doing things. I know I won't get caught in familiar traps. Thank goodness for all those "modest tests" because this is no longer modest. It's really my assumption come home to roost, and you never think that's going to happen. But I'm confident I can deal with it.

Stepping Back from Susan, Emily, and Peter: Keeping the Fire Burning

As Susan, Emily, and Peter's stories illustrate, furthering the work is most of all about finding ways to sustain a relationship with the assumption rather than becoming reabsorbed in it. Holding ourselves apart from it creates a space out of which new thinking arises, new choices appear, and new behaviors are tried. If our assumptions remain subject for us, if they are not examinable, then they hold together a system with which we became well acquainted in the work of building our initial four-column mental machine.

The Big Assumption (such as "If I am not continuously available, then I will not be valued or loved," or "If I do things that people do not like, then they will not like me, and [by implication] if they do not like me or think well of me it will be Intolerably Awful!") fuels the third-column commitment (such as "I'm committed to never saying no" or "I'm committed to people liking me and thinking well of me"), which in turns supports the behaviors (second column) that undermine our first-column commitments.

In other words, our Big Assumptions hold a system together that creates ineffectiveness and immunity to change. We further the work of the internal languages by making the familiar strange and giving ourselves the chance to make the strange (the possibility that what we have taken as true is in some way a distortion) more familiar.

The technology of the four-column exercise is intentionally designed to give us reasons to want to disturb our Big Assumptions. It shows us how our Big Assumptions anchor our own ineffectiveness and our powerful immunity to change. It gives us a picture of ourselves pulling in opposite directions at the same time. These are not common or flattering self-portraits, but they are intriguing. Developing them may even be necessary if any deep change is to occur. Faced with them, we either turn away or move toward their exploration. It is almost impossible to do nothing.

But in the absence of a special context, it is far more likely we will eventually turn away. The stories of Susan, Emily, and Peter show us what can happen when that context has been experienced for increasing periods of time. Susan's story gave us a glimpse of carrying on the language work in a graduate course that met fifteen weeks for three hours. Emily identified her Big Assumption in an institute that met for two weeks, and then again for ten days four months later. She continued working on her Big Assumption on her own, periodically talking with someone from the institute, including one of us, for over a year. We interviewed Peter after he had been using the languages for his personal learning for more than three years. He and a colleague who attended the same program stayed in touch with each other around the work throughout those years. For each of these people, an alternative language community, even a tiny one, supported efforts to productively shake up and reinvent long-standing ways of being in the world.

Susan, Emily, and Peter all had thoughts about what specific qualities within their learning environment they felt were instrumental to their growth. Susan sees five contributing factors:

1. I felt accepted in the class, by colleagues and teacher. Who I was, was fine.

2. I was discouraged from venting the negative feelings I had about Jo by the structure of the class. Only late in the semester was

one permitted to "knock before entering" with unpleasant news. And, even if that unpleasant news were to be delivered, it had to be framed in terms of how *I feel* rather than how *you are*.

3. I not only trusted but respected other members of the group. I was open to what they might have to teach me. Where did this trust and respect come from? Since I'm not quick to offer it, I guess the answer must be that people had gained it, by their words and deeds. They exhibited characteristics in my pantheon of how people ought to be. I found them to be smart, caring, funny, sincere, and hard working.

4. I wanted to change and was looking for ways to do it. When I came back to school, one of my goals was to learn how to get along with people better. Rather than, as I had previously done, seeing my academic goals as limited to the arena of my own scholarly achievement (Grades 'R' Us), I had interpersonal goals as well.

5. Before I actually felt differently (less judgmental of peers), I was willing to suspend my disbelief and change my behavior— e.g., I didn't run to a friend with my complaints, I didn't make subtly snide comments (or even faces) about Jo in class. Until I was able to find some kind of positive way to behave, I was willing to do nothing.

Emily comments on what she experienced as a powerful aspect of her holding environment:

I think about all the years of therapy that I've paid for. And why I could act on this only now. I think there was something very powerful about being in a group where everyone was doing this themselves. . . . The guy I did this exercise with, in his case he was saying that, in essence, he had sold his soul to be at a big-name institution and he was very unhappy with what they did to him and he was afraid—his assumption, in effect, was that he would be nothing if he left a big-name institution. And he almost came to tears when he realized it. At that level, having that from this guy who seemed like a pretty tough-skinned, knows-what-he-was-about guy, that was very unexpected. And seeing the impact of the process on other people, it felt like a communal experience as opposed to something you were doing yourself. Also, it was something about knowing that each of us would come back to revisit the assumption when we next met.

Peter sees the initial bonding experience with other participants in the professional development institute as a critical ingredient to his continued relationship with his Big Assumption work. He says:

> There were three or four people from the original institute whom I've been in touch with over the years. We phoned one another more frequently in the first year or so, and now we count on those few occasions when we'll see one another, like at a conference. Whenever and however we connect, we don't even necessarily talk about our assumption work. What we do is celebrate and re-celebrate our common experience. I know this probably sounds corny, but simply being in touch with them renews me and my confidence in myself as a leader in my institution.

What we hear Susan, Emily, and Peter telling us is that we need a "holding environment," a place in which to participate safely in the types of conversation that help us fully engage our investigations of the third force within us. The motive to disturb our own pattern of thinking is important but still just a spark; the first glimpse of our Big Assumption is, at best, tinder. In order to carry on the work, the spark must become a flame. The seven languages are intended to be a steady supply of oxygen to keep the flame burning for as long as our learning may need.

Further Reading

Kegan, R. *The Evolving Self: Problem and Process in Human Development.* Cambridge, Mass.: Harvard University Press, 1982.

Kegan, R. *In Over Our Heads: The Mental Demands of Modern Life.* Cambridge, Mass.: Harvard University Press, 1994.

Kegan, R. "Epistemology, Expectation and Aging: A Developmental Analysis of the Gerontological Curriculum." In J. Lomranz (ed.), *Handbook of Aging and Mental Health: An Integrative Approach.* New York: Plenum Press, 1998.

Kegan, R. "What Form Transforms? A Constructive-Developmental Perspective on Transformational Learning." In J. Mezirow (ed.), *Learning as Transformation: Critical Perspectives of a Theory-In-Progress.* San Francisco: Jossey-Bass, 2000.

Kegan, R., and Lahey, L. "Adult Leadership and Adult Development: A Constructivist View." In B. Kellerman (ed.), *Leadership: Multidisciplinary Perspectives.* Upper Saddle River, N.J.: Prentice Hall, 1983.

Kegan, R., Lahey, L., and Souvaine, E. "From Taxonomy to Ontogeny: Thoughts on Loevinger's Theory in Relation to Subject-Object Psychology." In P. M. Westenberg, A. Blasi, and L. D. Cohn (eds.), *Personality Development: Theoretical, Empirical, and Clinical Investigations of Loevinger's Conception of Ego Development.* Hillsdale, N.J.: Erlbaum, 1998.

Lahey, L., and others. *A Guide to the Subject-Object Interview: Its Administration and Interpretation.* Cambridge, Mass.: Subject-Object Research Group, Harvard Graduate School of Education, 1988.

Rogers, L., and Kegan, R. "Mental Growth and Mental Health as Distinct Concepts in the Study of Developmental Psychopathology: Theory, Research and Clinical Implications." In H. Rosen and D. Keating (eds.), *Constructive Approaches to Psychopathology.* Hillsdale, N.J.: Erlbaum, 1990.

Souvaine, E., Lahey, L., and Kegan, R. "Life After Formal Operations: Implications for a Psychology of the Self." In C. N. Alexander and E. J. Langer (eds.), *Higher Stages of Human Development.* New York: Oxford University Press, 1990.

Chapter Nine

Running the Social Languages

In Chapter Five we introduced the first of the social languages, the language of ongoing regard, and distinguished this direct, specific, and nonattributive way of communicating our experience of appreciation or admiration from the customary praising, stroking, or handing out of warm fuzzies and "attaboys." So how might one promote such a language?

Furthering the Language of Ongoing Regard

Consider what might happen, just as an example, if at every meeting that we have occasion to lead—meetings of staff, committee, project group, team, department, faculty, or division—we regularly began by opening the floor for any expressions (direct, specific, nonattributive) of admiration or appreciation that anyone might like to deliver.

The worried responses we usually get to this suggestion are along these lines: "What if I do this and no one has anything to say and I'm greeted with a long, awkward silence?" "But what if one person never gets thanked?" "Do we have to do this publicly, in a group? Too touchy-feely!"

Let's take each of these worries in turn.

The Role of Leaders

What if nobody has anything to say? In our experience this has actually never happened, but even if it did, we believe it would still be a net gain for a language-shaping leader. Even if no one has anything to say today, you still exercise your leadership on behalf of conveying that this is something that can go on here at work. This is something that has a place to go on if it wants to, if not today then perhaps tomorrow.

When you create a place for something, it is remarkable how much more likely the thing is to occur. This is what we mean by leading a language community. The idea is not only that leaders should pay attention to how they speak and what they say but also that leaders have the opportunity to create places or channels for unusual forms of communication between and among all the members of the community.

Consider, for example, most people's attitude toward staff meetings in general. Their anticipation of meetings at work is cheerless at best. "Oh, great," they mumble to themselves or to each other as they enter the meeting room, "another department meeting. Just what I'd like to be doing!" This eye-rolling response to the prospect of yet another staff meeting is part of what we call the "privileges of followership." Followers are entitled to grouse about business as usual. Leaders are not. Leaders do not have the privilege of rolling their eyes and saying, "Well, that's another two hours I'll never have back in my life."

They do not have this privilege because they are running the meeting. How would you feel, standing in line to board an airplane, to hear the person behind you say, "If the Good Lord had really wanted us to fly, He'd have given us wings!" and, when you look behind you, you see the speaker is the pilot? The leader doesn't have this privilege—but this doesn't stop many leaders from inappropriately exercising it.

As leaders, our recognition that people aren't so thrilled to attend our meetings should actually draw our attention and provoke our concern, in much the same way that frequent party-throwers would register the comment if a friend told them, "Look, this isn't easy to say, but I'm your friend, and if I don't tell you, who will? Most people aren't that thrilled about coming to your parties."

Of course, a meeting must deal with the pressing business at hand, no doubt about it. But a meeting actually is also an occasion of special opportunity. Here we all are together. Usually we are spread out, each engaged in his or her piece of the operation; but for this brief period here we are, all together. Try to arrange such a thing on an ad hoc basis; the task of coordinating everyone's schedule is usually a nightmare. A gathering of the whole is an opportunity not merely to handle the momentary business of the day, but to re-mind (and re-spirit) ourselves as to what is most important to us collectively, what we care most about, what we stand for or are up to in the bigger sense. Not having at least a small portion of every meeting given over to this regenerative purpose is a terrible squandering of a leadership opportunity.

But this is exactly what goes on in meetings (even efficiently run meetings) every day. Ironically, though we are living in the midst of an extraordinary revolution in communication technology at the turn of a new century, certain arts of communication—well-practiced at the turn of the last century and still crucial today—are withering on the vine. Chief among these is the art of hospitality, or hosting in its deepest sense, too little practiced or appreciated by most American leaders today. The art of hospitality is about a great deal more than a warm smile and a remembered name.

Have you ever attended a social function, for example—let's say an occasion in honor of someone's happy event—where things may have gone something like this? The food is tasty enough; the drinks are cold enough; people have pleasant enough chats in twos and threes. But no one summons whatever it takes to clink two glasses together, quiet the separate private conversations, and draw us from many fragments into one common experience by uttering even a few words about the guest of honor or how happy we all are to be there for her. We leave the party, drive home with a friend or spouse, aware in some way, often wordlessly, that the event seemed incomplete. Perhaps we can even identify what was missing: that not just the guest of honor but we ourselves were deprived of the experience of being part of a whole, directing its collective attention to a purpose, to a moment, to a person we care about and came to acknowledge.

More often, we may not even know exactly what is missing, why the occasion seems not fully to be an occasion, or why even the temporary stimulation of the signs of festivity are a poor substitute for the satisfaction of deeply integrated, purposeful social experience. We sigh and move on. Today, at the beginning of this new century, we may try to shrug off our dissatisfaction with such an event. But anyone who has studied the social forms of American life of a hundred years ago would tell you that if people had experienced then the same kind of unacknowledged occasion so commonplace to us today, they would have regarded it as exceedingly bizarre.

Whatever the communications advances of the last hundred years, they do not include our mastery of the human arts of hospitality. On the contrary, these arts are in increasingly short supply, and it's hard to see how any of the wizardry in communications technology that will characterize the twenty-first-century workplace can make up for leaders' limited hosting capacities that were prevalent in the nineteenth. The essence of hospitality is located not in a warm smile and a hearty handshake but in the ability to create a meaningful shared space in which our attentions and intentions are aligned.

When a leader makes a space at the beginning of a meeting for any expressions of appreciation or admiration that anyone may wish to deliver, she uses the special occasion of our all being together to communicate that this is a place where we can give such support to each other. This is a place where, in addition to getting on each other's nerves and disappointing one another (as inevitably people do at work), we can also appreciate and admire each other—and say so. This is a place where we can not only efficiently dispose of the functional administrative tasks before us, or keep the train running on time, but be viscerally reminded why we want to be on this train in the first place.

By creating a preexisting channel for such communication, the language-shaping leader invites people, whether they know it or not and whether they make use of the channel or not, to bend their minds toward awareness of their experiences of admiration or appreciation. Like practicing a spiritual discipline, one finds—even in the midst of all the ways work continues to be troubling or difficult—that one sharpens one's capacity to feel genuinely appreciative or admiring—a vitalizing way to feel.

By creating a channel for expressing this experience, the language-shaping leader increases dramatically the chance that others besides oneself benefit from having such an experience. After all, if there are no regular opportunities for assisted delivery of such communication, what is likely to happen to our experience of appreciation and admiration? What is the likelihood that you will actually let anyone know about it? Even though you are aware of this experience, our best guess is that you are still not likely to tell the person about it if a public channel does not exist in your workplace. Consider what you have to overcome to do it. You need to track the person down, ask for a moment of her time, perhaps say whatever introductory words you need to in order to establish some meaningful context for the communication itself, and then actually deliver the communication.

This is a lot to ask. It is a big barrier to expect people to climb over. Most of the time, even aware of our feeling appreciative or admiring, we are unable to transcend this barrier. After all, we are nearly always busy. Other people and things demand our time. There are still two dozen phone messages and e-mails we haven't answered yet. Most likely, we will not deliver the communication. What a shame. It is a loss for the community, a social event that never occurred. Leaders, acting as language shapers, can work against such losses.

What About the Person Who Doesn't Get Regarded?

"What about the person who doesn't get admired or appreciated?" people ask us. "Isn't there a risk there?" It's interesting that this question so often comes up when we first introduce the idea and never recurs once a language of ongoing regard is up and running. There seem to be two reasons for this. First, the question reflects how different a role such communication plays if it is a one-time event versus a feature of the ongoing flow of professional conversation (the essence of a language form). If such communication is rare, it is a big deal who gets appreciated and who does not on that special, unusual occasion.

If it is part of the usual conversational process, there is no stigma associated with not being "regarded" on any one occasion. "Don't you do as much harm as good by leaving people out?" is a common and appropriate response to prize-giving activities (such as Employee of the Year). But the language of ongoing regard is not a prize-giving activity. It is not distributing a scarce or limited resource but creating an expanding resource.

What if someone were never to be regarded publicly or privately throughout the life of the language? This seems unlikely (in practice, people don't tell us about it). But even if it did occur, it might be useful information for the nonregarded: "Do I provide so little opportunity for people to have an experience of my work? Why doesn't it register as admirable or appreciable?"

But the more important reason this concern about not being acknowledged or recognized seems to diminish with the actual practice of a language of ongoing regard is that, properly engaged, there is no prize-awarding dimension to the communication at all—not one-time prize awarding, nor even frequent prize awarding. Remember, especially by way of the injunction to be nonattributive, that such communication is about the speaker rather than the person the speaker is addressing. Once it becomes clear that a language of ongoing regard is providing people information about the sender more than the receiver, the question of who gets thanked seems to diminish in importance.

Do We Have to Do It in Public?

Sometimes people say to us, "Well, yes, OK. But do we have to do this in a public group? That's not my kind of thing. It's too touchy-feely." Or they say: "Doing this with my group? I personally would be quite comfortable with it, but I think immediately of a few of the people I work with, and they would be just climbing the walls! They'd go nuts! 'Yuk,' they'd say. 'How did I suddenly find myself in a therapy group?!'"

We find these perfectly understandable and welcome responses. Our answer, of course, is that you do *not* have to promote the language of ongoing regard in a public group. What we are suggesting is that appreciation and admiration deserve a thicker life in your work setting, and that this particular suggestion, like all of our suggestions, is no magic bullet, but merely an example of a way to create and preserve the language under discussion. As you consider the intentions behind all seven languages, you probably find occurring to you your own ways of realizing these intentions. Our suggestions are just examples, possible concrete ways of realizing an abstract ambition.

But before you quickly dismiss the suggestion of opening such a channel in a public group—either because it makes you uncomfortable or you think it will make others too uncomfortable—we wonder if you've ever considered that the way you are currently running your group meetings is also likely to be making some people uncomfortable.

Have you ever considered that the less personal, button-down, business-efficient way of operating in a work group, however well established it may be as a notion in your work setting, has long been making some members of your group uncomfortable? Or have you ever considered that the bantering style of jocular informality that has become the language norm in your work setting has long been making some members of your group uncomfortable? You're probably right that any new possibility for how we talk to each other at work will make some people uncomfortable, but how should you, as a language leader, regard such a prospect?

In today's climate of being more respectful toward issues of diversity at work, an admirable and noble ideal has begun to take shape: that all differences come to feel comfortably included in our work setting. This is a moving aspiration—and one day perhaps it will even be possible to realize it. Until then, we have a much more modest aspiration to suggest. Maybe one day all differences will come to feel comfortably included at work; in the meantime, we'd like to see the discomforts *more evenly spread around.*

Surely some people will feel uncomfortable with *any* change you initiate at work, but should this be a ruling criterion for nixing your plan, when there are inevitably also people uncomfortable with the status quo? The seven languages appeal to and discomfit a variety of personal styles. We think what is more important to avoid is not the prospect of making a person uncomfortable but that of the discomforts having to be borne always by the same people.

In fact, our own experience is that when we work with groups and give the members an opportunity to communicate their ongoing regard (as directly, specifically, and nonattributively as they can), they often end up surprising themselves with how much they have to say. Standing at the front of what is sometimes a large group of people, able to see all their faces at a glance, we often wish each of them could momentarily trade places with us to see the pleasure, the softening, that registers in the faces as they witness their colleagues being appreciated and admired.

No, such communication doesn't have to happen in a group, but when it does there are all sorts of compounding benefits. We note that people derive something of value merely from being present for such a language, even though they are not themselves the one receiving the communication, in the same way we enjoy watching a hard-working colleague open a gift she has been given at work.

The public nature of talking this way in a group does not have to replace or diminish private communication. On the contrary, delivering such communications in a group can actually increase the incidence of such communications occurring privately between people at work (in their talking with each other, in little notes that get passed back and forth, in e-mail messages). Public life, carefully attended to, can alter and enhance the nature of private life; this is what wholesome civic leadership and vital public ritual have always been about.

Many of us are so cut off from spiritually nourishing relationship with value-driven communities that the very word *ritual* means to us *empty or automatic formulaic behavior.* This is not the definition of *ritual.* It is the definition of desiccated ritual, ritual cut off from any meaningful, vibrant source. A ritual can be a vessel in time by which we remember what is important to us. Inspired leadership helps the members of a group to "re-member," to once again take out membership in what the group values and stands for; to "re-member," to bring the members back into one cooperating whole. Leaders as language shapers look to the possibilities for remembering in the forms of our speech.

We recommend promoting the chance to communicate ongoing regard in a public group not merely to generate a greater number of appreciations or admirations, as if it were only an efficient means of production, but to help remind the group—by being in the presence of such a language—that this is a place where what I do matters to others, and what others do matters to me.

Leading the Language Community

Effectively leading a language community does not necessarily mean being its lead talker. In fact, although we recommend that leaders of meetings create a channel for broadcasting ongoing regard, we also suggest that they themselves stay off the channel, at least for a while, especially if they are both the leader of the meeting and hierarchically in a superior power relation to the other members of the group.

If the appreciation or admiration comes from the boss, it can be heard less as a report of the speaker's experience (even when delivered nonattributively) and more as a subtle directive. Ongoing regard can end up feeling more like subtle social engineering or manipulating massage (intended or otherwise) if its source is the boss. A weird element of control creeps in and corrupts the space. Only after it is clear that the leader is not creating the channel of ongoing regard for the purpose of managing by reward can the leader communicate her own ongoing regard occasionally and then possibly be heard as just another colleague.

Thus, the leadership idea of helping to create and sustain relatively rare forms of speech at work is not about being the one who actually utters the form of speech the most. It is more about creating channels or contexts for such speech to be uttered by others—a lot. It is about enhancing a richer form of peer-to-peer communication; it is not about the leader ratcheting up his volume of attaboys.

One thing that seems to be true of most leaders we meet, regardless of age, gender, type of organization, or part of the country, is this: they are tired. Leaders are very tired. We've come to a stunningly brilliant realization about this: most leaders tend to feel they are working too hard because (are you ready for this?) they—are—working—too—hard!

When we as leaders take it upon ourselves to be the source, the initiator, the creator of all the good things we want to see happen at work, we are working too hard. We would do much better (for our own health and for that of our organizations) if we spent more time bending an ear toward good things already wanting to happen here, waiting to happen here, but still highly unlikely to happen unless a leader creates a context or channel for them to happen.

People actually *want* to let their colleagues know how what they do matters, and they want to hear from their colleagues how their own choices and behaviors matter to them. We can tell this by all the energy that is released when a channel for ongoing regard is created. Even so, as we said at the start of Chapter Five, nearly every organization or work group we meet astonishingly undercommunicates the genuinely positive regard that is hiding underground like an untapped fuel.

Here is a source of productive energy that does not come from the leader. It won't tire the leader if the energy is widely expended. But it is only potential energy; it requires leaderly initiative to make it kinetic, to help it be released into the setting.

Furthering the Language of Public Agreement

In Chapter Six, we introduced the language of public agreement, suggesting it was as different from regulation by rules as ongoing regard is from praise and prize giving. We also said that the language of public agreement was a means for fostering organizational integrity as well as generating observable internal contradictions for use in our learning.

But how exactly might we further creating and practicing this language in real work life (as opposed to merely illustrating it)?

Real organizations and work groups are, of course, more complicated than the simulated one we created in Chapter Six. They almost always have a history. They are already in business. Whatever salable product they have produced, they have also inevitably generated a set of systemic dysfunctions and troubled interpersonal relationships. They have produced reputations that accompany people's formal titles, conferred authorities, and public functions. They have produced problems.

This makes establishing a language of public agreement more difficult—but not at all impossible, as we have seen in our own experience. In fact, the reality of an organizational history that is inevitably not trouble-free can also serve as an aid, not simply a barrier, to the task. A history at work means people can already point to problems, and as we will see, those problems can be a resource for fashioning public agreements.

What Agreements Are Already Shared Among You?

Since our position is that you can begin to assess the state of organizational integrity (as distinct from the collective private integrities of the individual members) by looking for the public agreements that exist and how violations are treated, we begin by asking a group or work team a disarmingly simple question: "What agreements are shared among all of you?" This usually leads to recognizing how thin (and inconsequential, with respect to daily life) are the genuinely groupwide agreements they share.

People have no trouble identifying private agreements, usually among a small number of people ("Well, I have a signed letter of agreement with my CEO [or senior partner, or dean] that spells out the terms of my employment." "Richard, Helen, and I have agreed we are coowners of all the data in our research project and accordingly that all our names will be on all publications drawn from the data."). There's nothing wrong with such agreements, but they have nothing to do with the shared groupwide life of the department or organization.

A next common response is that people refer to policy manuals and governance structures, as in "All employees will treat information about the manufacture and distribution of our products as proprietary; they are not to be shared with any individual or organization outside the company, and requests for such information should be reported to your direct supervisor." Or "Regular reports and evaluations will be submitted in a timely fashion." Or "Faculty will not ordinarily be allowed more than two consecutive years leave." Or "A two-thirds vote of the partners will be required in order to. . . ."

These are certainly groupwide rules and norms; to the extent that incoming employees actually have the experience of assenting to them and all parties hold them in awareness, they do constitute a set of agreements. Of course, many if not most employees, new or old, have never had a single collective experience that involves their assent to the agreements; and most employees experience no closer relations to these agreements than Soviet citizens did to a dead but describable Soviet Constitution that sat in a drawer somewhere and had no real role in their civic lives.

More important, the issues these agreements typically address protect organizational life at its boundaries and extremes, which, though necessary and valuable, are not where most of a person's organizational life is lived (how much of what I do at work is related to guarding proprietary information, or not exceeding a two-year leave?). So even though they cover supposedly important matters, they are also in another sense inconsequential; little of the stuff of day-to-day organizational life feels their impact or follows from them.

Finally, if this kind of agreement is violated, the violations are addressed privately, in an adjudicatory or behavior-corrective context by one's superiors, rather than publicly in a learning context with one's peers.

After referring to the private agreements and the policy manuals, the last realm that people sometimes refer to (in attempting to identify what kinds of agreement are in place) is what we call the "sorta" agreements ("Well, I guess we sorta have an agreement that we will keep each other informed about. . . ." "I think we have an agreement, sorta, that we can modify usual compliance with that policy if. . . .").

Once these sorta agreements are suggested, it is not usually necessary for us to speak to their limitations. Someone else in the group does it for us.

"We *do*?" says someone increduously.

"I didn't know we had any such agreement."

"Yeah," says another; "neither did I. I think it might be a good idea if we *did*, but judging from the way a lot of people operate around here, it'd be hard to say we have such an agreement now."

"Well," says the initial suggestor, "I always thought we did. I've always acted as if we did."

It becomes pretty clear, pretty quickly, that a sorta agreement, however fondly regarded by the person who believes in it, is no real public agreement at all. It's usually a piece of someone's private integrity—a someone who has deluded himself into believing his own value is more widely shared than it actually is.

Recurring Problems as Skunkworks

If the state of public agreement is customarily thin, how can we thicken it? Our preferred route is to convene an unusual brand of conversation about ongoing, recurring problems in the life of the group or organization. The usual brands of such conversation are— if in private, among friends—some version of NBC and BMW talk (the language of complaint), or—if in public—some verson of earnest troubleshooting and problem solving. We propose neither. Rather, we are interested in using the occasion of ongoing, recurring, problems as a "skunkworks," a source of novel, experimental organizational "products"—namely, provisional public agreements.

"Let's trust," we suggest, "that chronic problems admit of no simple solutions. If they did, you would long ago have produced them. Let's further assume that for chronic problems to be successfully engaged, some people will need to change not just what they do but what they believe. Changing people's beliefs—about themselves, about their colleagues, about their workplace—takes time (so we need the patience to enter a process, and should not expect overnight results); and it takes support (so we need to build new organizational structures that surround and hold onto not just 'the problem' but potentially changeable persons whose beliefs create and sustain the problem). Those organizational structures are what we mean by *public agreements*. We create them not so much to solve problems as to let problems solve us."

Rooting the public agreements in ongoing, recurring problems ensures that they are related not to the rarer boundary issues taken up by personnel policy manuals but to the commonplace yet highly significant stuff of daily worklife. The first step in such a conversation is to identify a juicy-enough problem (it's long-standing, it matters, it comes up often). The second step is to create an agreement around it, much as we did in the EPCOT simulation in Chapter Six. The third step—more like an ongoing walk than a step—anticipates that the agreement will be violated and builds a curriculum for transformational learning around the violations. Let's take a quick look at each of these.

Step One: Identify a Juicy Group Problem

Sometimes the problems that come up are hierarchical in nature; say, both the boss and the subordinates are in the room, and the subordinates identify a problem they see emanating from above. (This is a far more promising place to start than the other way around, and it requires bosses who are willing to listen to their employees' difficulties.) Sometimes the problems are lateral. We'll give you an example of each.

A leadership team of a complex, multidepartmental organization to which we consulted includes the CEO, department heads, and various officers with cross-departmental responsibilities. The department heads and the cross-departmental vice presidents are of equal rank; all report to the CEO. The department heads identify a juicy problem (long-standing, matters, frequent) they have with the CEO:

> You frequently make clear, both in word and in deed, that you place a high priority on supporting the departmental mission and initiatives each of us has put together and is leading. And you *are* supportive, lots of the time. But there is this one kind of thing you frequently do which you may not realize has the effect of undermining our leadership and the pursuit of our initiatives. That is, you frequently make a decision unilaterally or set a precedent through your public resolution of some problem which—while making perfectly good sense on its own terms—has the effect of working against what one or another of us is trying to do in our own units.

This leads to an animated conversation, the purpose of which is not to solve the problem or blame the offenders (after all, if there are no prior agreements there can be no present violations) but instead to clarify the problem by illustrating it, and testing to see if there is agreement about what is happening and its effects. In this particular case, the leader, after reviewing a few examples, readily agrees that his moves have the unintended effect of undermining not only the leadership of his department heads but also his own genuine first-column commitment to support his heads as higly self-initiating leaders.

He also notices that, in nearly all cases, the examples his department heads bring forward are situations where he felt compelled to act unilaterally because something had to be done in a time frame shorter than the week or more that is often required for the collaborative, collateral decision making they all agree they prefer.

The whole group demonstrates why this is not a simple problem admitting of a simple solution. First, the CEO says, "Much as I do not want to undermine our department heads, and much as I prefer collateral decision making, I do have to be honest and say, unapologetically, that in my role I do feel that I must on occasion take unilateral action, and I am unwilling to submit every decision to a deliberative group process." Second, the rest of the group agrees that the CEO should have this prerogative, and that they would want it themselves if they were the CEO.

Step Two: Create an Agreement

Having agreed the problem does exist—the things people say happen do happen, and the costs people say these things incur are acknowledged—we shift to exploration of whether there is even a single agreement the group might want to make that they believe can have a favorable impact on the problem.

After a lot of conversation, not unlike that in the EPCOT simulation, the group comes to an agreement in the following manner. The CEO acknowledges (1) if he can receive clear information from a department head in a timely fashion as to how specifically an anticipated unilateral initiative on his part could negatively affect the agenda of a given department head, he will want that and might modify his plan as a result; and (2) in those instances where he does anticipate taking a unilateral action, he can usually wait forty-eight hours before acting (the department heads have initially asked for only twenty-four hours, and the CEO, in a spirit of cooperativeness, has suggested he could even wait longer).

The agreement this leads to comes to be known as the Forty-Eight-Hour Window Agreement: the CEO agrees that before taking contemplated unilateral actions he will inform department heads of his intentions (they end up doing this by e-mail) and wait forty-eight hours before finally deciding and acting. The department heads agree they will not treat such communication as a general, "What do you think of this?" request but only respond with "I wish you wouldn't" *if* they can identify the specific aspects of their own leadership they believe are compromised by the CEO's planned action, and how it does so.

The department heads want the CEO to know how his plans can undermine theirs; the CEO wants to open the door to getting this information, but he does not want to commence a protracted back-to-the-drawing-board contemplation of a general issue around which he feels fast unilateral action is required. The agreement seems to all parties a promising way of aligning their respective needs, and they are pleased with it.

We'll return in a moment to the fate of the Forty-Eight-Hour Window Agreement, but first let's use the same group as an example of a nonhierarchical problem and the agreement which it spawns.

Another problem quickly agreed to, and easy for the group members to illustrate, grows out of the fact that some people (the department heads) have leadership responsibilities over a given subentity, while other people have leadership over institutionwide functions (the case for the cross-departmental vice presidents; for example, one is essentially a business manager, and another is in charge of professional development and evaluation across all departments). The different nature of what they are leading means they are not each confined to their own organizational space. They overlap. The VP for evaluation, for example, is in and out of the territory of every department head.

Sometimes the VPs are troubled by the feeling they are encroaching, which inhibits their fullest range of motion; yet our subsequent discussion of a specific example shows that department heads do not feel at all encroached upon. In other instances, the department heads *are* offended by what they feel is an invasion of their turf; yet subsequent conversation shows the VP has no idea she is violating some boundary. (After all, where there have been no agreements there actually can be no violations.)

The VPs and the department heads, accordingly, create what they come to call the Are-You-at-Ease Agreement, reflecting a shared conviction that if people find themselves doing business in a spatial or functional territory outside their own domain they should check with the leader of that domain to find out if he or she is "at ease" with what they are doing or planning to do.

This may sound like a simple and obvious enhancement (many of our agreements do), but were it to be observed (or even if its nonobservance were to constitute a public violation) it would actually represent quite a change for the leaders. (In actual practice, we doubt any agreement addressing an enduring dysfunction turns out to be simple vis-à-vis its observance.)

Let's consider one last example from another setting, a second lateral example. A group of faculty members at a professional school are lamenting about the poor quality of the evaluations they receive from the field supervisors who monitor the students' practice and internships. "It's so rare that any of them go into any depth, and rarer still that any of them are critical," one group member laments. "The students don't get the feedback they need, and at the end, when we are considering not graduating the weakest students four years after they've entered, we lack a paper trail that documents problems we know have been there all along."

This kind of NBC or BMW conversation continues with no language of responsibility for the problem until one brave soul enters differently: "I agree about the poor quality of the field evaluations. But, speaking as an advisor who gets copies of an advisee's evaluations from the field and from all course instructors, I'd have to say that our own evaluations of our students are equally thin and avoid saying critical things. When the Internship Readiness Committee, or the Graduation Committee, meets to consider a hard decision about a marginal student, it's the quality of our own evaluations as course instructors—their noncommittal nature especially—that gives us the most problems. There's five times more evaluations from us than from the field. The student has been reading these evaluations as saying 'You're doing OK' when really the student is not; the teacher knows the student is not, and the teacher sort of means to be saying the student is not, but doesn't! The field supervisors are not the only villains in this story. And they're not here in the room. We have a big piece of the action, and we're here in the room."

This is greeted with a lot of appreciative laughter of self-recognition. "And I'm not saying I'm any different," adds the truth teller. "When I'm behind the wheel of my car I curse the jaywalking pedestrian; when I'm a pedestrian, I jaywalk. When I'm the advisor I look at a collection of skimpy, issue-ducking evaluations and wonder why you all can't do a better job; when I'm the course instructor, with thirty-five evaluations to write, I whip right through them." (More appreciative laughter)

Eventually, the group makes a shared, public agreement to write fuller evaluations, and especially not to dodge the difficult ones with thin or vague language (the "voluminizer agreement," it is called, after the women faculty explain to the men that a voluminizer is a kind of makeup that makes thin lips fuller).

Step Three: Following the Fate of the Agreement

Moving from the problem (step one) to a public agreement (step two) commences this language and by itself can be an energizing activity. But unless there is a clear structure for staying in relation to the fate of the agreements (step three), the language dies of disillusionment ("We say we'll change, but it's business as usual"). Raising the expectation of greater organizational integrity and then not delivering makes the familiar disintegrity that much more disappointing.

Once agreements are made, two things can be almost guaranteed; both are valuable and both need a good welcome. First, there will be instances in which the new agreement is kept, and second there will be instances in which it is violated.

The language of public agreement is nourished by regular collective opportunities to check in on how the agreements are going. These meetings (or portions of bigger meetings) have as their purpose (1) celebrating organizational integrity, (2) refining the agreement, and (3) clarifying new internal contradictions for transformational learning. Let's look briefly at each of these.

Celebrating Organizational Integrity

During the check-ins people have an opportunity, first of all, to bring the language of ongoing regard into the language of agreement by explicitly, directly, and nonattributively appreciating or admiring their colleagues' contributions to an agreement holding. This experience—that the agreement actually has the power to reshape organizational behavior toward greater attentiveness, fairness, or effectiveness—promotes the feeling of organizational integrity.

The department head says to the CEO, "I appreciate so much your giving me the chance to show you why, if you approved that request, you would undo the past four months." The CEO says to the department head, "I admire the concise, bottom-line explanation as to *exactly* why you want me to reconsider." One faculty member says to another: "I found what you wrote about Julia's problems with linking the conceptual to the practical in her writing very helpful, and I think she did, too. Her next year's teachers, and I as her advisor, and Julia herself, all have a much clearer sense now of the goal regarding her writing."

These communications celebrate specific behaviors, but the bigger object of celebration is the members' shared creativity. They have made something together, and they are keeping it alive; perhaps they are coming to rely on its strength or stamina to survive in their work environment. They may even come to experience their work environment as a place where something can grow, and that they can have something to do with this happening.

Refining the Agreement

Of course, all the conversations during the check-in are not going to be celebrative. As members review actual practice relative to the agreements, they may decide that certain alterations to the agreement itself, or additional refinements, are needed. A group with a come-to-me-first agreement may decide it wants to appoint an ombudsman who can be a sounding board prior to coming to "me" first. Another group even decides it wants to publish a list of preferred modes of coming to "me" first: if you need to "come to" Enrico, you check the directory and see that it says he "would prefer face-to-face conversation from the start"; if you need to "come to" Rowina you see that she "would prefer voice-mail, e-mail, or written note first."

The group that makes the voluminizer agreement adds a feature, saying that advisors who find a written evaluation too thin or vague are encouraged to let the faculty member who wrote the evaluation know what kind of further information is needed. "Advisors should not feel reluctant to ask, or that they are being out of line for asking," is the main message in this further agreement, which is especially helpful for junior faculty who are unlikely otherwise to seem to be criticizing a senior faculty colleague.

Transforming Violations into Contradictions

But perhaps the most important function of the check-ins is to create a curricular (as opposed to punitive) space for conversation related to violations of existing agreements, behaviors that no one feels reflect the need to modify or refine the agreement but instead reflect individuals' opportunity to further their own learning. If people are willing to engage their own violations in a spirit of personal learning (as opposed to remorse or Mao-era confession), the others in the group usually find they can also make a space that goes beyond recrimination. In operation, this amounts to willingness to fold one's violations into the four-column technology of the internal languages.

For example, several faculty who are party to the voluminizer agreement concede at a check-in, when an advisor brings it up, that their evaluations of some students were sugarcoated or avoided the critical things they know should be in their reports. Since each of these faculty members is an ongoing member of a smaller learning group, they agree to pursue exploring their violations in those groups and report back at a later agreement check-in.

Here's what one of them says. (There's shorthand lingo that obviously requires your being familiar with the internal languages and the four-column technology of earlier chapters.)

Well, here's where I've gotten to with my not keeping the agreement regarding my evaluation of Martin. So my first column, obviously, is my commitment to our creating better evaluations, as good as we'd wish the field supervisors would produce.

And my second column, also obviously, is that I'm prone in these very difficult cases, like Martin, to gloss over the hard parts.

Now for the interesting stuff: the strongest fear I got to in considering altering this behavior is that I believe Martin (and the two or three other students with whom I also tread lightly) would give me negative evaluations if I really said what should be said. And I've seen what happens around here when you get poor evaluations from the students.

I've seen what happened to Norma, for example, when she stuck to her guns on thesis committees and required rewrites when material did not reach the very standard we would all have agreed was minimal five years ago. There's lots of pious lip service around here from the administrators about how we should not compromise our standards, but the evidence is that if you do uphold your standards and your ratings start to go down in the evaluations you get viewed negatively by the administration. The student-as-customer thing starts to take over.

One dean called Norma in and asked her if she wasn't being too hard on the students. And then students stopped asking her to be on their thesis committees and she had her contract cut because she wasn't being on as many committees as she was contracted for.

It's ridiculous to tell teachers they should uphold high standards and then essentially require them to be an attractive, desirable "purchase" by the student consumer. I've seen it happen with doctoral theses, and I'm afraid the elective courses are the next place it's going to happen. If I get tougher with Martin and the others, the word is eventually going to go out that I'm too tough a grader and people aren't going to take my course.

The administration is going to say out of one corner of its mouth that it supports the voluminizer agreement and out of the other corner my contract is going to be cut because not enough students are enrolling in my elective classes.

So my third column is, "I'm committed to not developing a reputation for being too strict." So there's the contradiction: I'm committed to fuller, more truthful evaluation, and I'm committed to not putting myself at risk by losing my popularity! My Big Assumption, of course, is that if my popularity suffers, the deans will not back me up, and I'll get screwed. Stay tuned. I'm going to work on this assumption, and I'll keep you posted.

This may strike you as an odd way of dealing with violations. No prostrate *mea maxima culpa*. No punishing wrath. Not even a guarantee the offender will abstain from repeating his offense.

But notice he *is* taking an unusual degree of responsibility. He is committed to a kind of examination of the very assumption that holds the contradictory equilibrium in place. This equilibrium creates the offending behavior; his immune system prevents his behavioral change.

It is true that egregious or damaging behavior cannot wait for the internal changes that lead to self-initiated change; those behaviors may require unilateral leaderly intervention, mandates, and consequences. The problem, however, is that most violations are not of this sort; yet most organizations have learned no other way to respond than externally imposed suasion or silent seething.

Most organizations, as we have said, do not foster agreements; they impose rules. They usually learn quickly that there isn't sufficient energy in the system to monitor and respond to all violations of these rules, so they tend to act unevenly and rarely enforce them. All of this contributes to the ineffectiveness, unfairness, and inattentiveness that breeds organizational disintegrity.

Ironically, a language that fosters internal learning about our failures to keep our agreements—which may seem nothing like the lean, mean, whip-cracking machine we first conjure up when we imagine an effective, attentive, and evenhanded way of addressing violation—might be a far more powerful way of promoting organizational integrity. The changing that people do because others make them costs an organization a very dear price and is much shorter lived than the changing people do because they have first changed their minds.

Furthering a Language of Deconstructive Conflict

Some of the agreements a group wants to make may have to do with how its members handle conflict itself (for example, the come-to-me-first agreement). But the prior view people may hold of the possibilities or dangers inherent in conflict necessarily conditions the particular agreements they would think to make.

In Chapter Seven, we introduced the language of deconstructive conflict, suggesting it is as different from constructive conflict as the language of ongoing regard is from praise and prize giving, or the language of public agreement is from regulation by rules.

The deconstructive approach to conflict contrasts with both a destructive approach (tearing down) and a constructive approach (building up). It suggests that behind the apparent virtue of the latter there lurks an unquestioning certainty about the truth of one's own evaluation or judgment. What *constructive* often means in practice is, "I must find a sympathetic, supportive, timely, and effective way to instruct the other." What a constructive approach is actually building up, unrecognizedly, is a truth-claiming relationship to one's own evaluation or judgment. In contrast, a deconstructive approach seeks a form of engagement that neither discounts my evaluation nor prematurely assumes its truth.

In contrast to the picture of a clash of personalities (the destructive approach) or the generous teacher helping the student into the light (the constructive approach), the deconstructive approach actually preserves elements of each of the other two. From the so-called destructive approach, it preserves the value of the clash; from the constructive it preserves the value of two people engaged in a relationship oriented to learning. It brings these together by encouraging both parties to be learners, and to convert their conflict from an unproductive clash of personalities into the potentially productive clash of ideas.

How might we actually further a language for deconstructive conflict in our work lives? Let's ground our discussion in a real experience of "disturbed difference" (our umbrella term for a host of conflictual experiences, including disagreements, arguments, taking personal offense at some action or inaction, negative evaluation, critical assessment, and dissatisfaction with the quality of a peer's work or contribution).

You Are Jamie

Assume for the moment that you are Jamie, a teacher with many years of experience at Emerson High School. You have a lot of respect and fondness for Lee, an appealing, enthusiastic, talented, idealistic young teacher at the school. You admire Lee's gifts as a teacher and capacity to relate so well to the students. You also have some mild, general concerns that Lee has not yet clearly worked out the professional role of teacher in relation to the kids, and you wonder if Lee is clear about the distinction between a friendly professional and a professional friend.

More specifically these days, while Lee is working so intensely directing the student play, you are concerned about Lee's relationship with a student in the cast. Lee has gotten into the practice of taking Pat home each night after play rehearsal. You have occasionally seen parents picking up their children from play rehearsal and, you believe, taking special note of a young student and a young teacher of the opposite sex heading off together in the night.

You don't for a moment suppose that Lee is having a sexual or romantic relationship with Pat, but you do believe the situation doesn't look good, for one thing. You believe that people in public positions must avoid not only wrongdoing but the appearance of wrongdoing. You worry that a talented teacher may unwittingly be in a position that could damage effectiveness. You worry that the student, Pat, could find the situation confusing. You worry that other students, by way of those in the play production, could start rumors that would be hurtful to Lee or Pat, or that other students could feel Lee has favorites.

The whole situation looks and feels bad to you, and you'd really like to see Lee discontinue the practice of regularly being alone with the student each night after rehearsal. You'd like Lee to have Pat arrange alternate transportation home. "Surely there is a better way for Pat to get home," you think. You know that you and

Lee have a trusting relationship, and you feel that you can and would like to talk with Lee. Your sense that something is terribly wrong here does not abate, so you decide to deal with your "disturbed difference" by talking with Lee. (As you can see, we purposely used names here that allow you to invent the genders of all the parties.)

Let's imagine some ways this conversation might go. Suppose Jamie notices she and Lee are the only ones left in the faculty lunchroom. She knows they both have a free period after lunch today, and that Jamie is never available after school because of the play, so she figures this is as good a chance as she'll have.

Jamie: (taking a chair next to Lee) Hi, Kiddo! Can I talk to you a sec?

  Lee: (pen in hand, looking up from some papers and an open textbook) Hi, Jamie! Sure—I don't get to talk to anyone these days. This play is taking up all of my time. If it weren't for this free period, I wouldn't be ready for this afternoon's classes.

Jamie: You're really working hard.

  Lee: (half attending to papers and text) Yeah, but I'm really enjoying it. It's going great.

Jamie: It's actually the play that I wanted to talk to you about.

  Lee: (still distracted) Uh-huh.

Jamie: I've noticed you've been taking Pat home at night.

  Lee: Terrific kid. Really starting to open up. Have you noticed the difference?

Jamie: Are you worried at all about how this looks?

  Lee: (turning fully to Jamie for the first time) What? Uh, no . . . should I be?

Jamie: Well, you know, Kiddo. People are funny about these things. Some people could get the wrong idea.

  Lee: (indignant) Has someone said something?!

Jamie: People talk. You know how a school is, like a small town.

  Lee: Look, Jamie, the kid just needs a ride. I don't think Pat could be in the play if I didn't provide a ride. There's only the mom at home and she has her hands full. People should mind their own business.

Jamie: They should, but . . . maybe you want to see if Pat can't get a ride with someone else? Just a thought. This is your first year; I'd hate to see anything ugly.

  Lee: Yeah . . . well . . . thanks.

Jamie leaves, feeling she really enjoys the opportunity to mentor the younger teachers and help them find their way in the minefield. Lee returns to her lesson preparations, feeling unsure she really wants to be a teacher if she has to spend her time thinking how everything *looks*.

Jamie's intention is to be constructive. But interestingly, in spite of the fact she asks questions ("Are you worried at all about how this looks?" ". . .you want to see if Pat can get a ride with someone else?") she is not really trying to learn anything. She is certainly not creating a conversation for the purpose of furthering her learning about her own beliefs or the meaning of her reactions. Perhaps she's trying to learn more about Lee's thinking, but if so, it's probably for the purpose of more effectively teaching her lesson.

Now, we're not suggesting Jamie has no important lesson to teach. Lee may well be playing with fire and what Jamie is trying to tell her is just what she needs to hear. However, since the majority of first-year teachers leave the profession before their fifth year, it might be preferable if promising young teachers like Lee were to learn a lesson like this one in a way that does not move them closer to the door.

In order for that to happen—for more promising young teachers to stay, or any important change to take place in how any organization or profession is doing business—it may be that the experienced members also have to change. Jamie may have something important to teach Lee. But Lee may also have something to teach Jamie. The language of deconstructive conflict does not suggest that every disturbed difference should be framed as an opportunity for reciprocal learning. But it suggests that unless such a language is available, no disturbed difference will be engaged this way.

You Are Lee

The language Jamie creates gives us very little chance to know what is going on for Lee. Let's drop you into her mind for a moment.

You are Lee, a young, energetic, drama teacher at Emerson High School, deeply committed to your students, idealistic, and effective. Many of the students admire you.

For the past several weeks, you've been engaged with directing the winter drama production, a demanding and exciting play, in rehearsal every day after school until 7:00 P.M. The after-school schedule is taxing for the students, and for their parents as well, who often have to come to school to pick them up.

Since you happen to live near one of the students involved in the production, you helped out by offering the student a ride one evening and now, more or less and with little ceremony, you've been taking the student home each night for several weeks.

And you really don't mind. The student, Pat, is a somewhat troubled but appealing young person who has been unhappy and unengaged in school. Though other teachers have tried, no one has succeeded in helping Pat get committed and invested in some aspect of school.

That is, until now. Pat has really begun, quite gradually, to come out of a withdrawn state while working on this play. Pat is conscientious and reliable, and beginning to interact well with some peers who are themselves beginning to appreciate that Pat has something to contribute. You have found that, in the informality of a car ride home, Pat seems to open up and talk in a way others have not found possible with Pat.

You are well aware you are not a psychotherapist, and these conversations are not of the sort that make you feel out of your depth. Moreover, although this involves a special commitment of time and energy on your part, you are keenly aware that a close relationship with a caring teacher can make a crucial difference in adolescence because you had exactly such a relationship as a teenager yourself and it was a lifesaver for you.

All in all, though you are a little tired these days, you are very pleased with the way both the play and your work with Pat is going. When you look at how each is coming to life, you think, "This is exactly the reason why I wanted to be a teacher!"

The Jamie-and-Lee Role Plays

Although the Jamie-and-Lee situation arose out of real life, we have invited hundreds of teachers to try to role-play a "conversation for reciprocal learning" arising out of Jamie's experience of disturbed difference. We give one teacher the you-are-Jamie segment of the story (or we give it to a group who collectively enact Jamie), and to the other teacher (or the other half of the group) we give the you-are-Lee segment (intentionally written so that no genders are identified, because for Lee this has nothing to do with his or her experience of the situation).

Even if we give the Jamie role players a copy of Figure 7.2, describing the difference between constructive and deconstructive language, the conversations the Jamies create have many of the features of the one we just depicted in the lunchroom. It turns out that it is hard to frame the deconstructive language. But, like anything else, the more practice people have, and the more parties that are practicing together, and the more people have a direct experience of the language in prior situations, the easier it is to enact it in future situations should one wish to.

As supportive as Jamie-in-the-lunchroom sought to be, we can identify several features of the conversation she framed that to us are problematic, and that frequently recur in the role plays.

First, she never got real informed consent from Lee that this was an agreeable time and place to have a conversation about a disturbed difference Jamie was feeling. (In our actual practice, *snagged* is common shorthand for disturbed difference, as in, "Would you have some time this week to talk with me about a snag I've run into with you?") In fact, Lee essentially said that the free period she now had was a precious and scarce resource and that she needed the time to prepare for that afternoon's classes.

Second, Jamie never really makes clear her contrary view. She asks, "Are *you* worried. . . ?" She says "others might . . ." (without ever being clear whether she has actually heard anything). She hints at her position without ever declaring it, owning it, taking responsibility for it.

Third, she never really elicits Lee's view. The conversation doesn't help us learn how Lee sees the situation. The you-are-Lee paragraph suggests there is a whole world of meanings behind Lee's choices, no piece of which is helped to appear in the conversation in the lunchroom. With neither Jamie's nor Lee's view made explicit, there is no real difference for either party to look at, only for them to experience. The conversation traps them into being subject to the difference; they cannot take the difference as an object of attention.

Trying to Engage Conflict by Making It Disappear

If we feel snagged with another and think to resolve or eliminate the snag by teaching the other, we are usually led to trying to drive out as much of the experience of conflict as possible (as Jamie's moves try to do). This is ironic because we end up trying to engage the conflict by driving it as far from view as possible.

But even when people are trying not to teach, and to construct reciprocal learning conversations instead, as in the role plays, we find (often with lots of group laughter and good humor) that our conviction that we are right, or our wish to find the key that will unlock the other's door and allow us to get them to change their behavior, creeps into our designs.

We don't think people should expect quickly to be perfect enactors of deconstructive approaches to conflict, or think they would need to be to enter into such a practice. We commend the spirit of seeking to design such a conversational space. Even the best architect can view her last building and see design flaws she will try not to repeat in the next project. If two parties have a prior agreement that they will try to create together a deconstructive approach to their snag, they can include in the conversation analysis of its design. The intention to learn (and not only to teach) when experiencing a disturbed difference is the first and biggest step to fashioning a new language available for use when the parties elect it.

But as a result of watching ourselves and others struggle with this new design, we have bundled a set of architectural suggestions into what we call our "baseball model" for deconstructive conversation. The baseball metaphor holds onto several elements at once and suggests a sequence of considerations others may find useful.

The Baseball Model for Deconstructive Conversation

If we think of the person who is aware she is snagged as a potential batter trying to get home, then our first thoughts go to the necessary preparations in the on-deck circle before she even comes to the plate. As Figure 9.1 suggests, there are three kinds of prior exercises we think useful. In some instances, they may actually unsnag us and the conflict disappears. More often, they put us in a better position to advance around the bases. We will be glad we did

Figure 9.1. Baseball Schematic for Deconstructive Conflict.

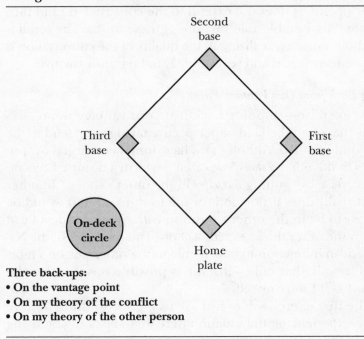

Three back-ups:
- **On the vantage point**
- **On my theory of the conflict**
- **On my theory of the other person**

them, and the people we end up approaching in deconstructive exercises will be glad we did them as well.

The three on-deck exercises involve stepping back from my vantage point, my take on the conflict, and my take on the other person. Just as people often take a few deep breaths before they go up to the plate, these three exercises involve a deconstructive set of deep breaths or purposeful pauses before engaging the snag with the other.

You may have a better chance to evaluate the usefulness of these exercises by going through them yourself as we describe them. Think of a situation in which you are currently, or were recently, snagged with someone.

Each of the exercises is deconstructive in that it recognizes we can too quickly form key meanings that we then uncritically carry into exploring the conflict. We hold these meanings as self-evident truths. No matter how open we may otherwise be in the conversation, our openness does not extend to the constructed (and thus potentially "disassemble-able") nature of these truths. The result is that, without our even realizing it, the quality of the conversation is largely predetermined and very unlikely to be transformative.

Stepping Back from Our Vantage Point

The first exercise—stepping back from our vantage point—reminds us that often the kind of perspective taking we extend to the other is quite limited. Although we have long been urged to "put ourselves in the other's *shoes*," we often perform a distorted version of this exercise by "putting *ourselves* in the other's shoes." In other words, it really does little good for me to think what it would be like for *me* to be in the other's position *with my mind* unless I can be certain the other thinks exactly as I do. The real work of the Native American injunction to walk a mile in the other person's moccasins is to walk that mile—insofar as possible—as if I were the other, not as if I were myself.

So the first exercise does not ask us merely to think how we might be experiencing the situation were we to be doing or saying what the other, with whom we are snagged, is doing or saying. It asks us to imagine or consider what the other might be experiencing. Especially, it asks us to see if we can construct a different experience, as the other, from the one we might construct as ourselves. It asks us not so much to put ourselves in the other's shoes as to imagine ourselves as the other and only then to put ourselves in the other's shoes. If you want to try these exercises, set up a sheet of paper to resemble Notepad 5 and jot down a few thoughts in response to all three questions before continuing.

Of course, we have no idea if our guess at the other's vantage point is correct. The purpose of the warm-ups is not by themselves to get us on base, but to increase the chances of doing so. We increase those chances by creating relationships with our constructions rather than being captive of them.

Stepping Back from My Theory of the Conflict

The second exercise invites us to consider that we have, often without knowing it, constructed an interpretation of our conflict. It has been made out of experiences we have taken as data, although our

Notepad 5.

1. Stepping back from my vantage point:

2. Stepping back from my theory of the conflict:

3. Stepping back from my theory of the other person:

data may be less given (the literal meaning of *data*) than *invented* by us. Our facts may be wrong. Even if our facts are corroborated, there are multiple ways the same set of facts can be accommodated by an interpretation. We can both agree on the corroborated fact that 40 percent of our town's teenagers are not graduating from high school. But for me, this fact can lead to a calamitous interpretation, while for you (who have seen this number above 50 percent for decades; or who believe the other 60 percent are going to receive much better education if the 40 percent who should not be in school get out) this shared and corroborated fact can lead to quite a contrasting interpretation.

So the actual activity of the second warm-up (you may want to use, and add to, the structure of Notepad 5) is to jot down two kinds of answers:

1. What are the supposed facts I am bundling into my interpretation, and might any of them represent distortions?
2. How might some third party whom I greatly respect (and thus would not quickly dismiss) bundle these facts into a different interpretation of the conflict from the one I am making?

Again, we don't know that our own facts are inventions; we don't know that our interpretation is inferior to that of our imagined respected third party. We are just helping ourselves toward a deconstructed relationship to the conflict situation.

Stepping Back from My Theory of the Other Person

The third warm-up exercise reminds us that most of our snags are with others with whom we already have some history. Because we are automatic, can't-help-ourselves, meaning constructors, the reality of a history inevitably means we have already constructed a prior interpretation of (or theory about) the other person, generally. How much of our present and future experience of this snag—including our experience with the other should we engage him in language about the conflict—is already preconditioned and predetermined by this preconstructed theory of the other?

The quickest way to perform the third exercise (again you may want to keep track of this in your version of Notepad 5) is to ask yourself, "If any other person—including someone I like or respect— were to have done or said what this person did or said, would I be feeling differently? How so?" Exploring these questions may well help you distinguish how much of your construction of the present snag is conditioned by a preexisting default mode in relation to the other person. Default modes are automatic, but they are also constructed. They can be altered.

Sometimes, as we said, the warm-up exercises can make the snag go away. This, however, is not their primary intent. That intent—as with all warm-up exercises—is to loosen us up. In this case, it is not our muscles we are trying to untighten; it is our meaning making. Our meaning making has gone from a fluid, ongoing process into an identification with products—namely, made meanings. If we can loosen all this up a little, we will be more successful when we come to the plate.

So what are our suggestions for furthering a deconstructive approach to conflictual language with the other? As the baseball model suggests, we think of four discrete steps (or bases) that may be worth keeping in mind. Traveling these bases with us also helps clarify how different the objectives of such a language are from those of destructive or constructive conflictual language. What kind of resolution of our disagreement are we seeking? What does it mean to succeed when conflict is engaged deconstructively?

To clarify a trip around our base path, let's take a look at a real snag at work and the deconstructive language that was built to engage it.

Reggie's Story

Reggie leads a team of five faculty who have collective responsibility for a required first-year course in a clinical psychology doctoral program. The school's dean prides himself on the quality of the curriculum and the teaching in the program. Reggie and her faculty group have become intrigued with a more student-driven learning approach called problem-based learning, in which the theoretical concepts are taught through realistic problem-based cases that students must work through over several sessions, pursuing independent reading with the purpose of teaching each other the concepts they need to solve the problem.

Reggie's team has spent several months observing the method in a medical school setting, and they are all interested in bringing it to their clinical psychology program. Their search of the Web and other references has led them to conclude that no one has yet developed a set of problem cases that would serve their curricular purposes, so they are becoming aware that actually initiating this innovation requires considerable additional expenditure of time and creative energy.

They happily and eagerly take on the additional work of studying the method, training themselves in the novel set of teaching skills involved in the new approach, collaboratively creating the materials for a pilot case, and working it through with a guinea-pig class to see how it goes. All this preparation leads them to be only more enthused with their project; but they also recognize that it is impossible to carry it out without some commitment of additional resources from the dean.

The dean, in preliminary conversations about a variety of possible reforms, has expressed support for the group's project. When Reggie tells him they are ready to send him a formal proposal, he says he welcomes it. But a few weeks after they submit it, she receives word that the dean is unwilling to provide any additional resources to make the project work. The dean encourages Reggie and her colleagues to continue as they have been doing, gradually developing the project, which the dean says he supports. But no additional resources can be approved.

Reggie and her colleagues are disappointed and angered by the dean's response.

"How does he expect us to do this on top of everything else?" one group member says. "He says he supports the project," chimes in another, "and he wants to keep the school on the cutting edge, but he's not willing to put his money where his mouth is!"

Reggie on Deck

Reggie decides to consider the present state of affairs as a live conflict rather than a dead end. She enters the on-deck circle and takes herself through the three warm-up exercises. (We won't take you through the particulars of this here, but let's assume they help her calm down a little; they give her some hunches, or at least a curiosity, about various ways the dean might be making sense of all this; and they remind her that she is somewhat predisposed to think the dean will not back his words with his deeds. The exercises certainly don't resolve the snag for her or make her less interested in talking with the dean.)

Reggie's Trip to the Plate

She asks the dean if they can have a face-to-face meeting about the proposal and his response to it, and he agrees. They set a mutually agreeable time for the meeting. Here is how it goes:

Dean: I hope my response to your proposal wasn't too discouraging. I think what you and your team are up to is very exciting, and I hope you'll keep at it.

Reggie: We've done a lot of work getting to this point, just studying the method, seeing what goes into writing a case, and working it through with the students. They're excited about it; we're excited about it. We've learned a lot. But we've also learned how much more has to be done if we are really going to institute this next year. We need your help.

Dean: I'm all for the project. My only problem is with the money part. You've requested reductions in either next semester's teaching load or summer salaries. I can't do either of these.

Reggie: Hmm. I know you're saying you're supportive. I guess— are you saying this is just something that the budget does not allow?

Dean: I *am* supportive. And, no, it's not honestly about the budget. It's the principle. What you all are proposing is an exciting revision of the way you teach the Foundations course. You've been at it several years, and now you're thinking about what might be a more powerful way to engage our students in its purposes. I like that. I like it a lot. To be frank, this is exactly what I expect excellent faculty like yourselves to do. Instead of being stagnant, and doing the same thing you've become so comfortable with, you're taking a chance on changing. This is why we are a good school. But, to be blunt, this is just what I see is your job. You are doing your job, and doing it well. It should not just be new teachers who have steep learning curves and feel sometimes overwhelmed with the unfamiliarity of it all. It should be veteran teachers like yourself and your teammates. I applaud this kind of growth and change. But I don't think I should make extra provisions available. I don't think that should be necessary.

Reggie: Uh-huh. . . . Well, I have to say that is a whole different way of thinking about it. . . . If I get you, you're saying that we are doing our jobs and you don't think extra provisions should be handed out just for people to do their jobs. . . ?

(Dean nods)

Reggie: And I guess I can see how you wouldn't want a string of other faculty lined up at your door looking for more resources every time they decided to change their syllabus or some other such thing. . . ?

Dean: Exactly!

Reggie: OK, I think I get that. I guess I'd like to ask you, while we're discussing it, if there are any other kinds of problems you have with our project or our proposal.

Dean: (thinks for a bit) No, I think we've really covered everything. As I say, I'm all behind the project itself. I don't think I have any other concerns.

Reggie: OK, that's helpful to know. I've appreciated this, and I wonder if we can agree to keep thinking about this and talk again.

Dean: Well, I guess we can. But . . . I'm not too sure where we can go beyond what we've said.

Reggie: Well, how about this? I wonder if there's something you'd like me to give more thought to before we meet again, anything I can do, or find out, or consider further that you would want.

Dean: (thinking) Well, I guess the question I'd have is, you know, is there some way this can move forward for next year without summer salaries or a reduced teaching load? I like the proposal. Is there some other way my office can be helpful?

Reggie: OK, great. That's a terrific question, and our team will explore it before you and I meet again. And I'm wondering if I can also ask you to give something a little more thought before our next conversation.

Dean: OK.

Reggie: As I'm thinking about your concern, which makes a lot of sense to me, I find myself wondering if it might also make sense to distinguish between changes of a different scale. Might there be small-c-type changes that are properly seen as part of the faculty member's job and for which additional resources are not appropriate, and capital-C-type Changes that are really more in the nature of institutional reform, for which it might be appropriate for the school to invest additional resources? So I guess I'm wondering if you'd be willing to consider whether such a distinction even makes sense, and leaving aside which side of the line our project falls on, thinking about where such a line would be drawn?

Dean: Hmmm. OK, I'm willing to give that some thought.

Reggie: Great, then. Thanks for this, and I'll look forward to our next conversation. . . .

We can use this brief conversation to illustrate four discrete moves we recommend for furthering a language of deconstructive conflict. Although an ambitious conflict buster might come to the plate hoping to hit a home run and score a conflict-ending resolution with a single brilliant stroke, we recommend what in baseball is considered a less dramatic approach, the station-to-station offense, in which we give each base its due, stopping there long enough to secure the smaller agreement or resolution each base has to offer on our way home (see Figure 9.2).

Getting to First: You Agree I Can "Come In"

Let's call first base "knock before entering" (KB4E). It is a simple step to perform but often overlooked. It reminds us that no one likes to be intruded upon, surprised, jumped from behind. We don't advise engaging the deconstructive language by crossing into someone's space unannounced or unwelcomed. The resolution that gets us to first base is a mutual resolve to meet at an agreeable time in an agreeable place, to address the snag between us. Unlike

Figure 9.2. Four Goals in Moving Around the Four Bases.

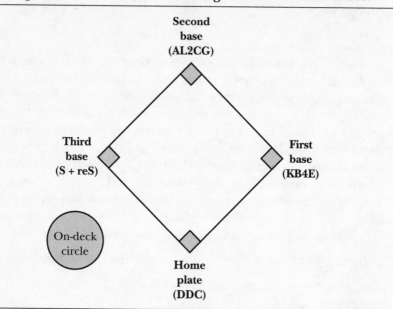

Jamie catching Lee in the lunchroom, before Reggie began her conversation with the dean he knew the purpose of the conversation, agreed to have it, and set aside a time and place for it to occur. Reggie knocked before entering.

Getting to Second: You Agree I Understand

Second base we call "active listening to clarify the gap" (AL2CG). This is a far more difficult step, and a counterintuitive one at that. Its purpose is to explicitly—even glaringly—declare just how far apart the two parties are. Unlike Jamie's understandable effort to keep invisible the distance between her position and Lee's, the resolution Reggie is seeking with the dean here is his agreement only that she clearly understands the contrary position he holds.

We know we have successfully reached second base when the other person stops using our name ("But, Bob . . .") at the beginning of exasperated or "patient" sentences meant to help us better understand his view, experience, or predicament. Note that

Reggie does not merely restate the dean's position; she *inhabits* it. Her words, which make his position even more explicit than he himself had presented it ("You don't want a string of other faculty lined up at your door. . . ."), arise out of her actively inhabiting his position as best she can, seeing how it might feel to be there, and then telling him something of what she imagines that feels like. This is what active listening is all about. It is one of the most valuable conversational skills a person can develop. It is not about parroting the other's words, a surface action. It is about the activity of empathically taking up temporary residence in the other's meanings and making sounds that let him know you are there. When he hears these sounds, he knows you get it.

Of course, it is one thing for a concerned therapist, parent, spouse, or friend to listen actively in this way to the upset feelings of a person one cares for. It is quite another to extend this kind of support to someone whom one is set against in a conflict sufficiently troubling that one has decided to engage the other in a conversation about it. Why would we support a position we don't agree with? By inhabiting the contrary position, don't we seem to be giving it even greater legitimacy? ("You understand it so well, it must be self-evident.")

Actually, active listening is not about supporting the other's position. It is about supporting the language space, so that a deconstructive conversation can ensue. It is about making the language space the holder of the competing positions rather than each person feeling he or she has to be the holder of his or her own position. "Active listening to clarify the gap," the work of the second base, does feel like the moment the two parties are furthest apart. It feels like a counterintuitive step away from, rather than toward, a goal of agreement.

But take a good look at a baseball diamond: when the runner moves from first to second, she has actually moved *away* from home base; standing on second, she is, measured in feet, further from home base than at any other point on her trip around the bases. Yet *no one scores without passing second.* Remember: deconstructive approaches to conflict do violate our familiar assumptions about what kind of resolution we might even want from conversation between the disputants.

Getting to Third: You Agree to Continue

We call third base "searching and researching" (S + reS). It is initiated with eight simple words, forming a request any person who considers himself reasonable would have a hard time denying: "Can we agree to keep thinking about this?" Buried in the question is the small, unique resolution we seek from this base. Again, we seek no large (conflict-ending) resolution from any base. Ending the conflict right away is actually not our goal. In fact, we'd like it to last long enough that the conflict becomes a vehicle for our learning. It is for the purpose of transporting ourselves in this vehicle that we take the trip around the bases. Once the vehicle is constructed, we can ride it for as long as the learnings to which it takes us seem worthwhile. Knocking before entering and listening actively to clarify the gap lead us to a place where, with a resolution to consider the gap further, we can convert the conflict into a dispute about ideas. The conflict persists, but productively.

Reggie and the dean do not just agree to the vague sentiment that they will ponder the matter further. They have assigned each other specific tasks, and accepted those assignments. Can a dean who does not provide financial resources still be in *some* way a genuine support? Is there some point where the size of a desirable change exceeds the scale of what it is reasonable to say is part of a faculty member's job description? Though it seems obvious there must be *some* kind of affirmative answer to both of these questions, even the slightest movement in that direction by either or both parties in this dispute constitutes a deconstructing of the truths each has been cherishing.

Getting Home: The Conflict Becomes a Seminar

So, in this analogy of ours, what is home plate? What does it mean here to score, to accomplish the goal? Having constructed the vehicle for deconstructive language, home plate is about driving the vehicle. It is where the future conversations occur, conversations that involve letting each other know what we have learned and involve additional reciprocal requests for further consideration of the new questions or issues that arise. Home plate is where the conflict becomes a seminar. The root of *seminar* is "semina," the Latin for seed. Deconstructive language seeks to convert conflict into a context where individual and organizational learning can grow.

What are the outcomes of these ongoing, overlapping seminars? This is not certain. The new course in Reggie's school either will or will not get created. Lee does or does not stop driving the student home from the play rehearsals. Visible things occur. But the language of deconstructive conflict increases the chances that whatever occurs does so because people have, if even a little, changed their *minds*.

Toward the Transformation Highway

Transcending the Limits of the Information Age

In Parts One and Two, we invited you to experience seven qualitatively different forms of internal and interpersonal discourse for transformative learning and leadership. We provided detailed case material and examples of these discourses, in Part Three, to illustrate a number of ways you can continue this work at the level of personal learning and organizational change. To conclude this book, we want to suggest how the rhythms and functions of this new learning technology can also be used to address vexing problems on the largest scale.

For the past fifteen years, we have been privileged to act as something like confessors to the professions. When we began we worked primarily with teachers, school administrators, therapists, and clergy. We feel honored to work with these very same groups today. And we are now as likely to find ourselves with physicians, Wall Street specialists, judges, management consultants, deans, or business executives. Afforded extraordinary access to the deep-down inner life of a widening array of professional groups, we have been struck by how frequently—in settings as diverse as medicine, management, or the schools—leaders are in the grip of a similar big problem, thanks to a limited conception of leadership and learning that is the unwitting heir of the information age.

It is an unusual opportunity to work across so many noncommunicating professional groups. We suspect that most people in any one of these professions have no way of knowing that their hardworking brothers and sisters in very different lines of work are struggling with the same problem as they are, what we have come to call the "maddening insufficiency of being well informed."

Imagine you are a conscientious and concerned physician practicing at this moment in history. There has never been more known about the human body, nor greater capacity for the practitioner to access this knowledge. There has never been such a storehouse of medical technologies or pharmaceutical sophistication. There has never been as much known about the way the relationship between doctor and patient plays a critical role in effective intervention. In so many ways, doctors have never before been so well informed with respect to diagnosis and treatment.

Yet if you go behind the scenes with many doctors, they take you to a repeatedly poignant place of frustration and even helplessness: the widespread *noncompliance* of patients in their own treatment. No increased capacity to diagnose illness correctly, prescribe proper treatment, or communicate sensitively with the patient has any effect on this weak link in the healthcare chain: many patients won't alter the behaviors that make them sick or take the medicine that will make them well. Imagine the frustration of a physician who has worked to master the necessary knowledge, who is profoundly well informed, in possession of the knowledge that should really make the difference—and who comes to discover its stymieing insufficiency.

To our way of thinking, this physician has met up with an immune system never taught in medical school. But it is one with which you are now familiar from reading this book. The key to unlocking its power may also be found in this new technology you have worked with here. For all the dramatic advances in scientific and medical learning, is it possible that medicine is in need of a new kind of learning and a new kind of leadership?

Imagine you are a management consultant or business analyst. You and your team members are frequently engaged to assess the operations and structures of organizations, to diagnose the constraints in present arrangements, and suggest new strategies and choices to help companies better realize their ambitions or even redesign their view of their purposes.

There may never be a business equivalent of the Genome Project, but within its own terms the accelerated capacity of management specialists to study organizations and their practices has been extraordinary. Because of new technologies and ever-more-sophisticated software, it is possible to array, sort, and quickly reassemble enormous amounts of data. Social science research and theory has dramatically increased the capacity of analysts to assess the dynamics of groups and individuals.

The most successful management consulting firms often do an extraordinarily good job of capturing a complicated picture of an organization or division after a relatively brief phase of immersion in that setting. The people who live in these organizations are frequently impressed at how well they have been seen. The advice, suggestions, bold new moves, and strategies the consultants develop with their clients' participation are in many cases greeted with appreciation, enthusiasm, and genuine commitment to pursue the new paths. These organizations often pay what would strike most of us as enormous fees for the consultants' services, and they pay them knowing that what they have received has been well worth the price.

This is why people are often disbelieving when we suggest that the consultants we have worked with are bothered or unhappy about something. After all, they leave the client feeling very well paid and well thanked.

But again, if you win the confidence and trust of many thoughtful and conscientious management consultants, you might be surprised to find that they are often *very* concerned about the insufficiency of being well informed, about the insufficiency of knowing what it seems is just exactly what needs to be known, of knowing what even the head of the client organization feels needs to be known: a considerable proportion of the good advice consultants proffer—they will tell you when they are being deep-down candid—is not followed, even when the client has been effectively involved throughout the process. The client welcomes the plans, pays for the work, endorses it as just what the company should do. And then nothing happens.

Is it possible that in spite of all the knowledge of what organizations need to do to succeed, a missing link is our lack of sufficient know-how to diagnose and disturb the immune systems that prevent organizations from making these very changes? Do consultants need to support a new kind of leadership in organizations to help them actually make use of their good advice? Do consulting firms themselves need a new kind of leadership to enact their own necessary changes in order to take on a new dimension to their work?

Imagine you are a junior high school teacher, a school principal, or a superintendent. You have already found your professional purposes lifted from your nation's backwaters to the front page of the newspaper and the first minutes of politicians' campaign speeches. You and your school are now being asked unfairly to provide almost every need a child has to grow up strong and healthy. You know that your school cannot do everything—but that it can do so much more than it does. You know your classroom, or school, or school system will only improve if the children within them find themselves in ongoing, powerful learning relationships and learning experiences.

Yet, as a distinguished colleague of ours at Harvard often says, "Ninety-five percent of what we need to know to provide excellent learning opportunities for all of our children is probably already known." We are already well informed, and it is maddeningly insufficient.

What we already know about what we need to do to make our schools more effective is a lot. We are asking teachers to reconstruct their roles, from being dispensers of knowledge and drillmasters to becoming learning coaches, hosts of learning communities, and creators of student-driven learning designs. Many teachers are not making these shifts, and people inside and outside the school world take this as an indication they are not really committed to the changes. But what if they are deeply and genuinely committed to these changes (in their "first columns")—yet are still not making them?

We are asking school leaders to become chief instructional officers and shift the bulk of their attention from technical, business, and political administration to the key activity that is the life blood of their organizations, namely, learning: the learning of students, the learning of faculty, the learning of their fellow administrators.

What if the many school leaders who are not making these changes lack neither the knowledge of the importance and value of the change, nor the commitment to make such changes?

Now, the irony in all three of these problematic stories—in the disparate worlds of medicine, management, and the schools—is that creating more knowledge—which is the triumphant activity of the twentieth century—may bring us no closer to solutions. Better health, better-running companies, schools that work—these are all admirable first-column commitments. They name, as do all first-column commitments, a version of the heaven we are trying to bring to earth.

The legacy of the twentieth century—the information age—has been the buildup of an extraordinary knowledge base around our first-column commitments. The difference between what we know now and what we knew one hundred years ago about, for example, the workings of the human body, complex social organizations, and the learning-and-teaching enterprise is impressive by any measure. But it is also undeniable that we enter the new century with legitimate concerns about our capacity to keep ourselves healthy, or to recreate our organizations and schools in a fashion that fulfills the demands and aspirations we have of them.

In our anxiety about the problems we face in spite of our extraordinary accomplishments, it would be natural to respond by doing more of the same, only harder. *Perhaps,* we say to ourselves, *if we can create not just an information highway but an information* super*highway*. . . . Politicians used to promise "a chicken in every pot"; now they promise "computers in every classroom"—and now, as then, the promise elicits exuberant applause as if one has been given a glimpse of salvation. But what if more of the same, only harder, only yields us more of the same? What if the new century must do something different than coast on the momentum of the information age?

The chronic smoker knows she is slowly killing herself, and she may be genuinely committed to her health despite her second-column behaviors. What good will better studies of the causes of lung cancer do her? The CEO knows his once-great company will be tomorrow's dinosaur if he continues to treat the new economy like an aberration that will disappear. How much is his own genuine first-column commitment to realign his organization advanced by a better forecasting model? The school principal may be genuinely committed to being an instructional leader despite all the second-column ways she stays out of her teachers' classrooms. Is another study on the benefits of student-directed teaching, or faculty professional development, or the misallocated way principals spend their time likely to help her disentangle herself from the preoccupations that divert her attention?

We are already the most overinformed, underreflective people in the history of civilization. We already have a twenty-four-hour news cycle, Internet newspapers, and continuous information about the day-to-day unfoldings of civic proceedings thousands of miles from our homes. A better-informed people is not necessarily a better-educated people. "In-*form*-ation" increases the store of knowledge in "the form"; e-*duc*-ation "leads us out of" the form itself.

Is it possible the twenty-first century needs a new kind of learning and a new kind of leader to help us in just this kind of leading out? Perhaps the new age will focus not just on the buildup of more knowledge but also on the fashioning of new relationships to the knowledge we already have. Perhaps we will learn to welcome and engage not merely our commitments to bring heaven to earth but also the competing commitments we have to keep hell *off* earth. (What are the smoker's third-column commitments and Big Assumptions? the dug-in CEO's? the principal's, in her inner office, far from the classroom?) Perhaps we will learn to move our Big Assumptions to a place where we have them, rather than the more customary place where they have us.

Perhaps we need leaders who are able both to start processes of learning *and* to diagnose and disturb already existing processes that *prevent* learning and change, the active, ongoing immune systems at work in every individual and organization. Perhaps you have learned something in this book that can help us begin building not simply an information highway but a transformation highway.

The Authors

Robert Kegan is the William and Miriam Meehan Professor of Adult Learning and Professional Development, chairman of the Learning and Teaching Department, and educational chair of the Institute for Management and Leadership in Education at the Harvard University Graduate School of Education. He lectures and consults widely within the United States and has been the recipient of numerous professional awards and honorary doctorates. The author and lead researcher of a theory of the evolution of adult competencies, his books *The Evolving Self: Problem and Process in Human Development* and *In Over Our Heads: The Mental Demands of Modern Life* have been translated and published throughout the world.

Lisa Laskow Lahey is research director of the Change Leadership Project at the Harvard University Graduate School of Education and cofounder and senior consultant at Minds at Work, a developmentally oriented consulting firm that works with businesses and schools to turn workplace problems and issues into opportunities for transformational learning. She received her doctorate in human development from the Harvard University Graduate School of Education.

Index

Kegan, Robert　　　　　　　　　　BF637
How the way we talk can　　　　K26h
change the way we work

Kegan, Robert

AUTHOR

How the way we talk can change　　BF637
TITLE the way we work　　　　　　　K26h

13506

2001

DATE DUE	BORROWER'S NAME